Attentive to God

Attentive to God

Spirituality in the Church Committee

KAREN MARIE YUST

Chalice Press.
St. Louis, Missouri

Cover image: Composite of photos by Image Club Graphics and Michael A. Domínguez
Cover design: Eduardo Martinez and Michael A. Domínguez
Interior design: Wynn Younker
Art direction: Michael A. Domínguez

This book is printed on acid-free, recycled paper.

Visit Chalice Press on the World Wide Web at
www.chalicepress.com

10 9 8 7 6 5 4 3 2 1   01 02 03 04 05 06

Library of Congress Cataloging–in–Publication Data

Yust, Karen Marie.
    Attentive to God : spirituality in the church committee / by Karen Marie Yust.
    p.   cm.
    Includes bibliographical references and index.
    ISBN 0-8272-0025-0
    1. Church committees. 2. Spiritual life. I. Title.
BV705 .Y87 2001
254'.6 — dc21   00-010285

Printed in the United States of America

For the Tuesday Morning Clergy Prayer Group,
whose belief in this vision of ministry
has served as inspiration and guide;
for Lois,
who refuses to believe that committee work
is just about marking items off an agenda;
and for my children,
David, Paula, and Michael,
who count on the church to make decisions
that will nurture them in faith.

Contents

Preface

Five years ago I began to experiment with a new way of leading church committee meetings. Instead of simply generating an agenda of tasks to complete, I tried to think about the theological concerns underlying the tasks and the spiritual and practical needs of the committee members attending to them. I was working predominantly with a Christian education committee then, and the members of that group arrived for meetings tired from parenting young children and worried that I would demand more time and energy from them than they wanted to give. Each of them wanted to "help out" with the administrative aspects of the children's church school program, but their vision for Christian education ended there. Most taught Sunday school, and most confessed a serious lack of biblical knowledge from which to teach others. We started and finished our meetings exhausted by the demands of our administrative responsibilities. Were it not for the underlying sense of obligation to contribute to the programs that nurtured their children, most of these folks would not have given up their evenings for such a burdensome experience. And I couldn't blame them for their long-suffering perspective. Committee meetings were a chore.

I cannot say that our Christian education committee meetings were transformed overnight by the introduction of worship, Bible study, and prayer into our gatherings. But as the committee began explicitly inviting God to attend our meetings and listening to God's voice in our deliberations, our sense of our work's importance in the life of the church increased, and our willingness to try new ideas and approaches did as well.

We paid more attention to issues of hospitality, intentionally nurturing one another with food, comfortable chairs, and conversation as part of our agenda. We established priorities according to theological values as well as practical considerations, and we began exploring ways to expand our understanding of Christian education to include persons of all ages. Our children's church school and adult education programs more than doubled in size over the next three years, a result in part attributable to the new vision and energy of the Christian education committee.

My colleague in ministry shared my interest in this new way of conducting church business, and together we introduced the idea of Bible study and prayerful reflection into the church council agenda. He also carried Bible studies and reflections I had created into committee meetings for which he was responsible. I wrote still more resources for congregations with whom I had long-term consulting relationships and, eventually, for the small church that called me as their sole pastor. My colleague, reflecting on how helpful these resources were for redefining the work of our particular church committees, remarked one day, "You ought to publish this stuff!" And so, here it is: a book about the theological and spiritual dimensions of committee work filled with more than fifty resources your congregation may use to transform its boards and committees into working groups attentive to God's activity and guidance in your community of faith.

Three congregations served as the primary test sites for these materials. Without the curiosity and commitment to faithfulness of committee members at Pleasant Street Congregation Church in Arlington, Massachusetts; Second Congregational Church in Winchester, Massachusetts; and United Church of Christ in Burlington, Massachusetts, these resources would not exist. I am immensely grateful to my friend and colleague, the Rev. Dr. Tom Clough, whose chance remark was the catalyst for seeking to publish my work and whose promise to buy the book was the impetus for completing the manuscript. His promise was echoed numerous times by the other members of the Tuesday Morning Clergy Prayer Group, and I truly appreciate their unwavering support.

I am thankful, also, for the students in my first "Introduction to Education and the Church" course at Christian Theological Seminary. Many of them took time to comment on this manuscript while it was "in process" and to try out some of the resources in their own congregations. All of them eagerly engaged some of these resources as a part of our classroom conversation together. To those who couldn't wait to call their board chair and read sections from the manuscript over the phone, I'm glad you now have the opportunity to use this book in your ministries.

Colleagues, church members, and students may choose to associate with writing projects, but family endures all things by default. My most heartfelt thanks belong to my husband, Brady, and our children, David, Paula, and Michael, who know firsthand my passion for the church and therefore have supported me in my efforts to create a book that we all hope will contribute to the health and vitality of congregational life. My thanks as well to my parents, Karl and Laureen, and to the rest of my extended family for their encouraging inquiries and expressions of pride. Only you know how truly amazing it is that this book has seen the light of day!

Chapter 1

Introduction

Every church, no matter how small or how large, does at least some of its work in committee. And because even the most homogeneous congregations have differences of style and opinion among their members, working in committee inevitably means that some process of decision making has to be developed. But where do churches look for ideas about how to do business? Much of the time, they look to the place where many committee members spend at least part of their day: the corporate world.

Corporate committees draw on several different principles in shaping their decision-making processes. Unless the committee is merely a perfunctory rubber stamp of the leader's decisions, it probably operates according to a "majority rules" policy. This is the most commonly known style of decision making, in part because it is practiced in electoral politics as well. When the "majority rules," decisions are made according to the wishes of the majority of committee members present. Even if almost half of a committee disagrees with a decision, that decision still stands if at least 51 percent of the members present voted to approve it. The negative implications of such a narrow victory—most prominently, resistance to a decision's implementation by a disgruntled minority—mean that many corporate committees work behind the scenes to generate sizable support for a decision before putting it to a binding vote. Such politicking can encourage healthy give-and-take among committee members, or it can foster a climate of secret negotiations and inappropriate pressure.

To support their "majority rules" policy, corporate commit-tees often utilize *Robert's Rules of Order*, a basic guide to parlia-mentary procedure first published in 1876. Developed by Henry Martyn Robert, an army engineer, *Robert's Rules* sets up a pat-tern of formal steps by which committees should accomplish their work. Basic to these steps are motions and their proper consideration and adoption. *Robert's Rules* also establishes crite-ria for committee bylaws and minutes. Not every committee that operates according to a "majority rules" style adheres closely to *Robert's Rules,* but most use some variation of this long-standing guide's rules of presentation and debate. For instance, committees are generally structured with chairpersons and secretaries or clerks, persons with special power and authority to shape the tone and style of committee discourse. Some officers use their power wisely and for the good of the whole; others view their authority as a license to manipulate and coerce less powerful committee members. Proposals often must be phrased as formal motions before they can be voted on by committee members. This helps to clarify the committee's intentions and contributes to good record-keeping, but it also requires a certain verbal skill that only some committee members have. And the vote itself is a crucial feature of *Robert's Rules.* Except in the case of unanimous decisions, there are always winners and losers.

The use of debate is another principle of corporate com-mittees. The ability of committee members to articulate and argue a position is highly valued. Often, the person who argues loudest and longest succeeds in winning the vote, or at least in delaying a loss. Committee members who are less-gifted speak-ers have little opportunity to voice their opinions or ideas. Em-phasis is placed on forceful presentation of one's own position rather than on careful listening and consideration of others' input. A good committee chairperson can prevent especially vocal members from dominating a meeting, but the debate format is seldom conducive to hearing from all committee members on a roughly equal basis.

The second model of decision making familiar to most church members is the system employed by families. All church members have experienced at least one version of the family decision-making process in their lifetimes, even if they are not currently part of a multiperson household. While every family personalizes this system, it is fundamentally a style of making decisions through delegation. Each individual in the family has the authority to make certain decisions within specific arenas. Sometimes these areas of authority are jointly determined, and sometimes they are assumed or assigned. Perhaps one adult family member makes routine financial decisions, while another member organizes the family's activities schedule. Or one person decides when and how the laundry gets done, and another is responsible for gift purchases. Some decisions may require a family meeting or consultation, but most are handled by the family member responsible for that aspect of family life. The failure of a family member to take responsibility for areas assigned to him or her may result in punishment or a loss of authority. And complaints about the way someone else handles a decision could lead to rifts in family relationships.

These two systems, then—the corporate and the family—are the models that most church members bring to the table when they gather for a church committee meeting. Even though they may not be entirely happy with the way these systems work outside the church, they assume that these same systems should be employed in the church's administration. And so they set about creating a decision-making process that mimics either the corporate or family model, or, most likely, becomes an awkward hybrid of the two. They miss the opportunity to create a new decision-making model that more fully honors the ideas of all committee members and the relationships between members while still getting the work done.

The purpose of this book is to suggest just such a new model and to assist congregations in implementing that model by providing resource materials that encourage and support their new way of operating. This new model turns to the scriptures and the traditional practices of the church for its inspiration. But this is not a model that loses sight of the practical needs of churches. Indeed, the practical aspects of running programs, recruiting volunteers, and evaluating practices are the body of this style of administration. It's heart, however, is the word of God made known to us in the Bible. If we don't allow the heart to pump its lifeblood through our bodies, our committees and the decisions they make and implement are lifeless.

Think back to the last time you participated in a church committee meeting. Did the experience leave you feeling drained and exhausted? Resigned or cynical? Unheard and misunderstood? Powerful and victorious? I've experienced all these emotions as I've concluded meetings over the years. But the emotion I've least experienced is that of exhilaration, that feeling of being empowered and uplifted by what I've just done. I've felt exhilaration coming out of worship and Bible studies, but rarely has my participation on a church committee elicited that sense of spiritual well-being that marks other aspects of church life. Is that because worship and Bible study are spiritual events, and church committee meetings are "business"? I've had church members tell me so. But I refuse to believe them. After all, Psalm 139 reminds us that there is no place that we can go away from God's spirit.

> Where can I go from your spirit?
> Or where can I flee from your presence?
> If I ascend to heaven, you are there;
> if I make my bed in Sheol, you are there.
> If I take the wings of the morning
> and settle at the farthest limits of the sea,
> even there your hand shall lead me,
> and your right hand shall hold me fast.
>   (Psalm 139:7–10)

Nowhere in this Psalm or in any other passage of scripture are church committee meetings exempted from God's presence and participation! It is our own separation of spirituality from "business" that leads us to reject the idea of spiritually uplifting committee meetings.

One way to bring spirituality and "business" back together is to redefine the purpose of church committee meetings. Instead of viewing meetings as sessions for reviewing "old business" and discussing "new business," we could view meetings as places where we engage in a process of discerning God's will for church life. This process requires that we acknowledge and welcome God's presence in our meetings as an essential contributor. No more perfunctory opening prayers by the clergy before getting down to "real" business! Prayers of this sort often serve more as an attention-getting device for committee members— sort of like flipping the lights off and on to signal the start of an event—than as a genuine request for God's active participation.

So how do we take God's presence seriously? The next chapter develops a theology of church committee work that is both scripturally based and practically feasible for the conduct of church business. This chapter sketches out a model of committee decision making that presumes that the purpose of church committees is to discern God's will for church life. It highlights biblical models of decision making and contrasts traditional committee practices (such as motion making and voting) with consensus-building practices. It portrays God as a potentially active member of every committee, from the board of Christian education to the trustees.

Chapter 3 suggests general methods committees can use to encourage awareness of God's contributions to their work. It offers practical instruction in the use of devotions, Bible studies, prayer, and specific group process skills that can assist committee members in maintaining a spiritual focus during meetings. Because every committee organizes its agenda according to its own needs and schedule, this chapter gives particular attention to how committee members can develop their own Bible study and devotional materials to address the particular concerns of each meeting.

Chapters 4 and following contain ready-to-use devotional and Bible study resources for the committees named in the title. Each chapter's resources are prefaced with a statement about the theological purpose of that committee. Each resource is preceded by a paragraph explaining why it has been included and followed by a paragraph offering suggestions for modification based on a committee's particular needs. Most of the resources included in these chapters have been tested in actual committee meetings, many of them in more than one setting.

God wants to be a member of our church committees. In fact, God is already present at our committee meetings. But our current models of decision making prevent us from hearing God's contributions to the discussion and experiencing the exhilaration of working with God in all aspects of our church's ministries. It's time we learned how to make God a real member of our church committees instead of relegating God to the non-verbal, non-voting, *ex officio* role so commonplace in our committee practices today.

In the Resource sections of the following chapters, abbreviations are used for three hymnals in current use:

CH–Chalice Hymnal
NCH–The New Century Hymnal
UMH–The United Methodist Hymnal

Chapter 2

A Theology of Church Committee Work

The primary purpose of every church committee is to discern God's will for church life. This may seem like a lofty, theological-sounding goal, but it is this purpose that sets church committees apart from committees in non-religious settings. A company focus group or departmental team may not care about God's desires, but the church exists to glorify and serve God, and therefore church committees must take into account God's expectations for their work. If church groups neglect to consider God's will, then they cease to operate as bodies of Christ, for to be bodies of Christ requires that churches acknowledge their dependence on Christ's leadership by acknowledging the one who is their head. And how can we be led by Christ if we do not ask what God would have us do? Whether we are deacons planning for a Christmas Eve service or outreach committee members deciding how to spend our budget for this year, we need to ask ourselves, What would God want? Otherwise, we may just be putting on a good show or behaving generously without doing all within our means to testify to the full depth and power of God's love.

Discerning God's will is an intentional practice of looking for, recognizing, and engaging in God's activity in the world. Discernment assumes, first of all, that God is indeed active in our world. It rejects the popular cultural viewpoint that human beings are responsible for all that is good and successful about our lives and our communities and instead sees God's hand in acts of justice, hospitality, and kindness. Like the Hebrew prophets, who interpreted natural disasters, wars, births, and vocations in terms of divine activity, church groups that practice discernment choose to interpret their own personal and communal lives in theological terms. Like the early church, which attributed healings and other miracles to divine intervention, discerning Christians see God's hand in the workings of medical practitioners and social justice groups. It's not that these events cannot be explained in other ways. It's that a discerning church *chooses* to see God's presence in all that happens in the world. It chooses to explain the world in theological terms, rather than to simply accept the world's non-religious explanations as the whole story. Thus, a Red Cross worker comforts a family displaced from their home by flooding, and the typical viewer of the nightly news sees a caring individual at work. But a discerning Christian sees God's comforting presence in the Red Cross worker's actions and gives thanks for God's loving care. It doesn't matter whether the Red Cross worker is a Christian; what matters is the viewer's understanding of how the world works. Those committed to a process of Christian discernment look at the world and see God at work in all that is.

It's easy enough to see God at work in benevolent actions, but harder to see God's hand in something like the stock market or banking practices. Yet a commitment to discerning God's will for church life requires that we expect to find God working in all areas of our lives. The Hebrew prophets had a much easier time interpreting financial losses and gains in terms of God's activity, in part because they often employed a theology of financial rewards and punishments tied to the Jewish community's obedience toward God. (Even when the Hebrew prophets saw that this connection was not always realized, they still assumed that divine intervention would eventually right the injustice of righteousness left unrewarded and evil rendered profitable.) The members of the New Testament church described in Acts 2 lived out their faith in God's financial presence by pooling their resources and trusting that God would provide for all through the sacrifices of all. They intentionally separated individual effort from daily provision and thus thanked God for their livelihood, rather than congratulating themselves on their industriousness. As twenty-first-century Christians, we need not interpret God's activity in the world in exactly the same way as the Hebrew prophets did, nor must we act out our faith in the precise manner used by the Jerusalem church in Acts. But we must engage in the same process of looking for, recognizing, and engaging in God's activity in the world. Only then can we claim to be God's people doing God's will.

In order to live out our commitment to see the world through theological eyes, discernment requires that we cultivate our sensitivity to the ways that God works in our world. Such cultivation occurs when we engage in practices that bring us into closer relationship with God and acquaint us more fully with who God is and how God relates to us as a beloved people. Worship, prayer, reading the Bible, reflecting, and doing justice are some of the practices that help us to become more sensitive to God's will.

Worship is both an act and an attitude. It is a practice of calling on God's presence and celebrating God's goodness through singing songs of praise and giving thanks through our offerings. It generally includes acts of proclamation (testimonies, sermons) and of community building (communion, greeting of peace). Worship sensitizes us to God's activity in the world because it focuses our attention on God and God's being. We are reminded in worship of God's majesty and of God's steadfast love throughout the generations, of God's demands on our lives and of God's great gifts to us. Worship calls on us to stand in God's presence and recommit ourselves to service in God's name. It reminds us that our God reigns in heaven and on earth.

Engaging in prayer is another method of sensitizing ourselves to God's work. Prayer can be practiced either alone or in community. It may be spoken or silent and may include elements of praise, thanksgiving, confession, intercession, and contemplation. Each of these elements encourages a different way of relating to God. Praise continues the work of worship and clarifies for us the nature of God. The Lord's Prayer illustrates this aspect of prayer in its opening words: "Our Father, who art in heaven, hallowed be thy name." The writer of Psalm 8 begins this prayerful hymn in a similar fashion: "O LORD, our Sovereign, how majestic is your name in all the earth!" When we praise God in prayer, we acknowledge God's greatness as the Creator, Redeemer, and Sustainer of our lives.

The prayerful element of thanksgiving orients us to our dependence on God for our well-being. When we ask God to "give us this day our daily bread," we acknowledge that God is the one who provides for our daily needs. The farmers, truckers, bakers, and grocers whom we usually think of as our providers of bread are really mediators of God's sustenance. It is in prayers of thanksgiving that we practice interpreting the world and its routines in theological terms.

The confessional aspect of prayer further grounds us in a healthy dependence on God. When we acknowledge our weaknesses and wrongdoing, we simultaneously acknowledge God's strength and ability to set us right. We cannot be discerning Christians unless we first admit that we are incapable of sustained faithfulness without God's help. For if we believe that we do no wrong, or that we have no need of God's forgiveness and guidance, then we live as if God's presence in the world makes no difference. Few of us would claim to be perfect, but more of us live as if our imperfections were benign and unimportant. The role of prayerful confession is to highlight the consequences of sin and God's promise of forgiveness and transformation. In the words of a traditional assurance of pardon, taken from the opening chapter of 1 John, "If we confess our sins, God who is faithful and just will forgive us our sins and cleanse us from all unrighteousness."

Prayers of intercession help us to make the move from looking for and recognizing God's activity in the world to joining God in that activity. When we ask God to intercede on our behalf and on behalf of others, we engage in a faithful action designed to further God's purposes on earth. Even if we can do nothing more than pray about a specific situation, we have acted to bring about the transformation of that situation, and that is in accordance with God's will. The apostle Paul's letters to the New Testament churches are filled with references to and requests for intercessory prayer. He writes to the Corinthians, "This is what we pray for, that you may become perfect" (2 Cor. 13:9). And to the church at Ephesus he writes, "Pray also for me, so that when I speak, a message may be given to me to make known with boldness the mystery of the gospel, for which I am an ambassador in chains. Pray that I may declare it boldly, as I must speak" (Eph. 6:19–20). Jesus counseled his disciples to pray for their enemies (Mt. 5:44 and Lk. 6:28). Prayer becomes an action to encourage righteous living, boldness, and forgiveness in these examples. It changes the attitude of the one who prays and opens up new possibilities for a transformed relationship with those who are the focus of prayer. Thus, it works with God to change the world.

Contemplative prayer, also known as the practice of silence, teaches us to make room for the voice of God's wisdom amid our own attempts to make sense of our lives. The writer of Psalm 46, speaking for God, admonishes us, "Be still, and know that I am God!"—for in our stillness, we remember that "God is our refuge and strength, a very present help in trouble" (Ps. 46:10, 1). Elijah, discouraged and fearing for his life, recognized God's presence in "a sound of sheer silence" (1 Kings 19:12) and opened himself to God's guiding voice. Amos, distressed by the Israelites' half-hearted religious observances and immorality, proclaimed that those who do not listen for God's voice will find that God no longer speaks to them: "The time is surely coming, says the Lord God, when I will send a famine on the land; not a famine of bread, or a thirst for water, but of hearing the words of the Lord" (Am. 8:11). We must quiet ourselves, expect God's presence in our silences, and offer our ears to God if we wish to know what God would have us do.

We hear God's word in our times of comtemplative prayer, and we encounter God's word when we read the scriptures. In the Bible, we encounter story after story about God's activity in the world. Genesis portrays God's work as creator and covenant maker, and Exodus gives us a thorough introduction to God's work as liberator. The prophetic books highlight God's actions as judge and redeemer. The gospels focus on the salvific work of God's word made flesh, and the epistles show how God continued to embody God's love through the formation of new communities of faith. The Revelation of John even provides us with a vision of God's actions at the end of time. All these stories remind us that God has been active in the past and is able to act as well in this time and place. When we read and study the scriptures, we learn about the ways in which God has chosen to act before, the principles that have informed God's actions, and the opportunities that God's people have had to work with God in transforming the world. We also discover cautionary tales about the consequences of ignoring God's presence and wise advice for living as people of faith.

As we read the Bible, we reflect on the scriptures' meanings and applications for our contemporary lives. We ask ourselves whether our daily practices and choices are consistent with God's expectations as they are expressed in the scriptures. We consider whether our relationships with God and others mirror the life-giving principles God has established and practiced throughout the ages. Sometimes we reflect on the scriptures privately, examining our own consciences and praying for God's guidance. Sometimes our reflections occur in a group setting, taking advantage of others' inspiration and experience as we interpret the scriptures and apply them to our lives. Both settings offer us opportunities to think about how God's past deeds are related to God's activities today and God's promises for the future. And our practice of reflection prepares us to act with God for the transformation of the world.

Finally, we cannot discern God's will without engaging in acts of justice, for it is in acting with God that we most fully experience God as active in the world. When we feed the hungry, clothe the naked, listen to the discouraged, comfort the grieving, set free those imprisoned by the injustices of our society, and otherwise follow the example of Jesus, we learn about God's will by doing God's will. We "put on the Lord Jesus Christ" (Rom. 13:14) and discover what it means to think and act with the mind of Christ. As we act with God, we are moved to envision new possibilities for future actions and different ways of being in the world. As we become beacons of God's love to the world, our light also enlightens us. The prophet Isaiah repeatedly proclaimed the connection between acts of justice and both personal and communal enlightenment. When we "loose the bonds of injustice," our light "shall break forth like the dawn" (Isa. 58:6, 8), and we become an enlightened people and "a light to the nations" (Isa. 42:6), just as God intended that we should be.

If we take seriously the idea that worship, prayer, reading the Bible, reflecting, and doing justice are essential to discernment, and if we believe that the work of church committees is to discern God's will, then our challenge as church committee members is to incorporate these practices into our committee work. It is not enough that we engage in these practices at other times and places. Certainly, we will worship on Sunday mornings and participate in outreach projects on Saturdays. We will pray at home and in prayer meetings, and we will study the Bible in Sunday school classes. We will reflect privately and corporately on the relationship of the scriptures to our daily lives. But if we do our church committee work in isolation from the more familiar spiritual practices of our faith, we risk losing the connection between "Spirit" and "business." To be faithful stewards of God's business, we need to keep God's spirit actively present in our committee work.

This means that we need to worship together as committee members. Committee worship can be as simple as lighting a candle to symbolize God's presence or as complex as a full-fledged worship service during the first part of the meeting. Some churches plan all their committee meetings for the same evening. In such a setting, everyone could gather for worship before breaking into their smaller committee meetings. So long as committee members resist the temptation to divide the evening into two unrelated segments, this practice allows for a familiar worship experience in the midst of conducting church business. A less-segmented method would place worship elements throughout a typical committee meeting. I have served churches in which the congregation's annual business meeting was conducted in the sanctuary, with hymns and prayers interspersed among the business items. While this method can become perfunctory, it has great transformative potential if practiced with genuine concern for worship. Hymns such as "Called as Partners in Christ's Service" and "The Church's One Foundation" can help a congregation make business decisions within the context of a biblically centered, loving community with a mission.

Church committees also need to pray together. Many committees now begin their meetings with a perfunctory prayer, often by the "designated pray-er," who is either a clergyperson or the committee chair. Such prayers serve to mark time more than to invoke the presence of God. Committees that want to reconstitute themselves as discernment groups need to pay attention to the five elements of prayer: praise, thanksgiving, confession (and forgiveness), intercession, and contemplation. Though not all these elements need to be woven into an opening prayer, every element can be a part of an evening's work. Opening prayers might offer to God the concerns that committee members bring with them to the meeting: anxieties about loved ones, tensions in their jobs, hopes for and frustrations with church life. Closing prayers might celebrate the work of the committee and offer thanks to God for guidance throughout the meeting. Prayers at any time might acknowledge the struggle to make faithful decisions and seek God's forgiveness for missteps along the way, as well as God's help in the future. Silent, contemplative prayer is especially useful as a committee finds itself nearing a decision or when decision making appears strained or stalled. At these times, pausing to sit quietly and await God's direction before proceeding helps the group to know that God has been included in their considerations. Such knowledge is just as important in decisions that seem to come easily as in more difficult decisions. For if God's guidance cannot be discerned in the simple choices, perhaps the decision is not one to which God calls us. The more faithful choice may require consideration of options we have not yet imagined. Contemplative prayer can help us to see when our decisions require more time and effort and can create a space where our imaginations more freely seek God's will.

No committee should underestimate the power of reading and reflecting on the scriptures together. The Bible is our primary source for information about God's hopes for the world, and within its pages are many stories that spark our imaginations and challenge our assumptions. While our contemporary issues may not be directly represented in these stories, the struggle to know God's will and make wise decisions is the central dilemma for biblical people. Remember the story of Jesus' being tempted in the desert? As Christ struggled to determine what he should do, he recalled the scriptures he had studied and learned in childhood. He used the Bible's teachings to confront the one who wished to distract him from his spiritual calling. All three synoptic gospels offer us insight into Jesus' reflection on how the scriptures should inform his daily life (Mt. 4:1–11; Mk. 1:9–11; Lk. 4:1–13). We, as church committee members, imitate Christ when we use the scriptures in the same way.

Doing justice together as a committee may seem to be a stretch for all but the mission/outreach board. But justice begins among ourselves. When committee members arrive at a meeting directly from work, is there something for them to eat for dinner? When a parent wants to participate on a committee, are provisions made for child care? These are issues of justice within our congregations. Showing hospitality to one another trains us to show hospitality to those outside our community. Jesus ate with his disciples as well as with the crowds who followed him around listening to his teachings and seeking his healing touch. And Jesus' call to his disciples included provision for their needs while they were traveling with him. The gospel of Luke reports that several of Jesus' female followers—Mary Magdalene, Joanna, Susanna—used their resources to provide for the group's needs (Lk. 8:2–3). The contemporary church community ought to do no less for those who serve the congregation and further its mission.

But doing justice as a committee practice of discernment need not limit itself to concerns within the group. Whenever a committee considers an expenditure or acquisition that will benefit the congregation, its members can also practice a justice-oriented ministry by asking, How will this use of money impact the poor, the oppressed, and the needy? In our global economy, every decision we make can have implications for justice. Attuning ourselves to these implications helps us to serve God by doing unto the least of these (Mt. 25:31–46). And there is no better way to attune ourselves to justice than by working with and for those in need of justice. Imagine how much easier it would be for committees to ask questions about the implications of expenditures after experiencing the poverty and need of those who are oppressed! If every church committee—no matter what their stated purpose—engaged in a mission or outreach project each year, those committees would carry into their deliberations the personal knowledge of what needs to be done so that God's realm might fully come on earth. Nothing can substitute for personal experience when it comes to learning to discern God's will from a perspective of justice.

When church committees constitute themselves as bodies for discernment, God becomes an active participant in their decision-making process. God is worshiped, engaged through prayer, encountered in the scriptures, discovered in daily activities, and sought as a founding partner in the realizing of God's realm. God's presence on committees changes them from business groups concerned primarily with practicality, frugality, and efficiency to spiritual discernment groups determined to be good stewards of all God's gifts within the congregation. Efficient processes, careful financial accounting, and practical considerations remain important, but they are means to an end and not the end themselves. And when efficiency, fiscal conservatism, or "common sense" seem to be in conflict with God's calling, a discerning church committee risks doing the foolish or absurd. They hold before themselves the theology of the cross and recall Paul's words to the Corinthians: "Where is the one who is wise? Where is the scribe? Where is the debater of this age? Has not God made foolish the wisdom of the world?" (1 Cor. 1:20). Sometimes the wisdom of God confounds our usual ways of doing business. In fact, with God as a member of our church committees, we end up with a new "standard operating procedure" designed to help us withstand the temptations of our age's deserts with the wisdom of Christ.

Chapter 3

Ways of Inviting God to Serve on Your Committee

Between my sophomore and junior years of college, I spent a summer as a short-term mission volunteer in Mexico City. Another college student and I were assigned to work with a small Salvation Army church in the heart of the city. On our first Sunday with the congregation, we learned that it was the pastor's practice to call on church members each week to stand and quote a scripture verse from memory and then to offer some thoughts on what the verse meant. This experience, more than any other, gave me a deep awareness of the fear that often grips people when they are asked to lead a group devotion or Bible study.

Many of us are afraid to talk with others about the Bible because we don't believe we know very much about the scriptures. Others of us, particularly pastors, may believe we are competent biblical interpreters, but we don't think we have the time to prepare committee study materials in addition to all our other responsibilities. Couple these perceptions with the fact that one quarter of the population is by nature introverted, and therefore somewhat less inclined to group leadership, and many committees may find that no one feels comfortable leading their group's devotional practices. So what are we to do under such circumstances?

We might begin by practicing the ancient biblical art of lament. A *lament* is a complaint paired with an expression of hope. The book of Lamentations in the Hebrew Scriptures is a collection of communal laments over the destruction of Jerusalem by the Babylonians. More than one-third of the Psalms are laments, including many of those attributed to King David. Laments begin by addressing or invoking God and then tell God about the problem suffered by those making the lament. In our case, we might begin simply: "God, we have a problem. No one in our group feels capable of leading our Bible study. We are frustrated by our lack of a competent and willing volunteer."

Having stated our problem, we would then move to the next phase of a typical lament—remembering God's past actions and expressing our confidence in God's ability to help us: "God, we know that you helped Moses when he felt inadequate to speak for the Israelites before Pharaoh. We know that you opened the eyes of the disciples on the road to Emmaus when they were confused and upset. We believe that you will help us as well." Next, like our biblical forebears, we would ask for God's assistance: "God, help us to develop the skills and resources we need to study and pray together. Help us to identify the gifts of leadership that we may not know we have. Give us the courage to invite you to our committee meetings even though we feel ill-prepared to do so." We would conclude our lament with an expression of praise, just as King David used to do: "God, with you all things are possible. Thank you for hearing our prayer. Amen."

Engaging in this practice of lament will not in itself teach us how to welcome God to our committee table each time we meet. But this exercise does serve two important purposes. First, it helps us to acknowledge the feelings of inadequacy that often paralyze our attempts to change our behavior. Such feelings are not peculiar to our time and culture. The scriptures tell us about Moses' anxieties and the confusion of the disciples on the road to Emmaus because the biblical writers knew that future generations would relate to their experiences. Even Paul confessed, "I do not understand my own actions. For I do not do what I want, but I do the very thing I hate" (Rom. 7:15). Although we want God to be a part of our decision-making process, we can have trouble realizing that vision. A committee lament helps us name our difficulties.

Secondly, the practice of lament reminds us that God has a way of helping us out of our difficulties and setting us on the path to new ways of being. When Moses complained that he had trouble speaking, God promised to provide the right words and identified Aaron as a resource as well. When the disciples on the road to Emmaus told Jesus about their confusion and disappointment, Jesus walked them back through the scriptures, explaining the words of the prophets. He then took time to fellowship and worship with them by breaking bread—both literally and symbolically—at the supper table. Our lament expresses our confidence that God will once again provide the skills and the resources necessary for us to embrace God's presence with us and to do God's work in the world. We need not be sure of the means of God's provision; we need only claim that we know God will provide for us just as God has provided for others in the past. In this way, a committee lament helps us see past our difficulties to the fulfillment of our hoped-for relationship with God.

We may start with lament, but we do not stop there. When we first learned to bake a cake or fix a leaky faucet, we began by picking a recipe or assessing the situation, gathering the necessary ingredients or tools, and giving it a try. We can use this same process to begin welcoming God to our committee meetings. The first step is to agree on a practice that we want to try. We might start with the practice that seems least intimidating to the group as a whole, or we might embrace a practice that particularly inspires one member. (In the latter case, the "inspired" member can act as a cheerleader when the process of implementation is rough.) The next step is to identify the skills we need to implement this practice. These skills might be general group dynamic skills, such as active listening, or more specific skills, such as an aptitude for biblical research. The third step is acquiring resources that will be helpful to the group as it implements and sustains its chosen practice. Resources can include books, objects like maps and candles, and even people outside the committee who have useful skills members of the group lack. The final step is trying out the practice we think will help us achieve our goal, learning from our successes and mistakes how better to engage in that practice the second, third, and fourth times we try it.

Let's say that our committee wants to engage in Bible study as a part of each meeting. The primary skills we would need are the ability to select an appropriate Bible passage, the ability to ask thoughtful questions, and the ability to listen carefully and compassionately. We might find that some members of our group already possess one or more of these skills or that we need to cultivate each of these skills in order to do Bible study well together. Skills come as gifts to some, and as the products of hard work to others. So let's consider how we could develop each of the primary skills that help a committee study the Bible fruitfully.

The ability to select an appropriate Bible passage requires two other secondary skills: the ability to identify significant committee issues and the ability to find Bible texts that relate to those issues. The simplest way to identify significant committee issues is to make a list of the committee agenda items for a given month and then to prioritize those items according to the amount of time and energy they are likely to generate in the meeting. The item that has the highest priority would be linked to the Bible study text. Alternatively, the Bible study could be linked to one of the general goals of the committee, which by definition are the guiding principles of all the committee's work. These goals may be stated in the congregation's bylaws or in a committee mission statement or job description.

Finding a Bible passage to link to an agenda item or committee goal can be as easy as remembering a Bible story from childhood or a memory verse from church school. However, not all of us come from backgrounds that included strong Bible teaching (or even church attendance), and even those of us who do have impressive biblical backgrounds do not always remember the location of a particular passage. So the ability to find an appropriate scripture for study depends more or less on our having access to a good concordance and study Bible.

A concordance is a book that lists key words from the scriptures and then under each word lists all the places in the Bible where that word appears. The place listings also reference the phrase from the text containing the word, so that the reader can decide whether the usage listed is the one she or he is seeking. The best kind of concordance for finding an appropriate text is an "exhaustive" concordance, or one that lists every word contained in a particular translation of the Bible. With a shorter, or abridged, concordance, the searcher's options are limited, and useful passages may be overlooked because the concordance's editor didn't recognize their significance. Also, because concordances have been made for a variety of Bible translations, our job will be easier if we choose one that matches our congregation's preferred version. That way, when we do happen to remember a useful passage, we can find it by looking up a key word in the concordance and reading through the list of places where that word appears until we see the phrase we've recalled. Some concordances have an index of significant words from other translations, making it even easier to find passages remembered from earlier study or memorization.

A good study Bible is also helpful because the margin notes list passages related to the ones being read. Some even contain topical "chain" references or information that tells the reader where to find additional passages on the theme of the first passage. A list of these topics is included as an appendix to the biblical text. These notes and references help us move from a passage that seems promising but doesn't quite address the issue we have to other passages with similar themes that may be more directly applicable to our concern.

Let's imagine that our congregation's governing board or council is meeting this week. On the agenda are some budget issues, reports from other committees, a discussion of space allocation for the church school, and a vote on a proposed behavioral covenant for church life. After reviewing all these items, we decide that the covenant vote seems to be the most important issue for this month. We get a copy of the proposed covenant and notice that communication, especially speaking politely and listening to one another, is a major theme of the document. A second theme is welcoming everyone into the life of the church by showing respect for one another. So we sit down with our exhaustive concordance and look up the words *speak, listen, welcome,* and *respect.* We read through the phrases under each heading, making note of the scripture references that seem interesting to us. Once we have several references (or we have exhausted the lists), we look up these references in our study Bible. We like the text in Ephesians 4:25–27, which reads, in part, "Let all of us speak the truth to our neighbors, for we are members of one another," but it doesn't quite capture the covenant's concerns. A footnote on verse 26 points us to James 1:19–20. There we find that verses 19 to 25 address the same issues of communication and respect that our proposed covenant does. We have found a passage for our committee Bible study.

Now that we have a text, we need to think about questions to guide our study. Good Bible study questions can help us do several things: They can help us identify the basic story or issues raised by a text, they can encourage us to think about the text in light of our own experience, and they can call us to respond to a text in ways that nurture our faith and contribute to the coming of God's realm. Seldom will one question assist us in doing all these things, and so we need not spend our time crafting the "perfect" question that will take our group from text to action in one giant step. The best plan is to develop a series of thoughtful questions that move us from a basic interpretation of the text and its relationship to our experience to a faithful response. We begin to implement this plan by reading carefully through our selected text—in this case, James 1:19–25:

> You must understand this, my beloved: let everyone be quick to listen, slow to speak, slow to anger; for your anger does not produce God's righteousness. Therefore rid yourselves of all sordidness and rank growth of wickedness, and welcome with meekness the implanted word that has the power to save your souls. But be doers of the word, and not merely hearers who deceive themselves. For if any are hearers of the word and not doers, they are like those who look at themselves in a mirror; for they look at themselves and, on going away, immediately forget what they were like. But those who look into the perfect law, the law of liberty, and persevere, being not hearers who forget but doers who act—they will be blessed in their doing.

If some parts of the text seem unclear, we can try reading the passage in a different translation; sometimes a different choice of words helps clarify an otherwise confusing point. For instance, the *New Revised Standard Version* (printed above) uses the phrase "all sordidness and rank growth of wickedness" in verse 21. The *Good News Version* translates this phrase, "every filthy habit and all wicked conduct," and the *New International Version* uses "all moral filth and the evil that is so prevalent." Each translation offers a slightly different idea of what the author of the book of James may have meant to condemn as undesirable. We can also consult a Bible commentary for ideas about what a particular phrase or passage means. By attending to our own points of confusion and looking for clarification, we discover the places where others are likely to have questions that seek answers. This helps us to develop questions for our Bible study that focus the group's attention on the basic story or issues of the passage. Three good questions for the James passage, then, might be, What kinds of behavior do you think James is asking his congregation to discard? What does James want the congregation to be doing instead? and Why does James think congregations should monitor their behavior?

Questions that focus on the text as it appears in our Bibles are "clarifying" questions. They explore the biblical author's intent in telling the story, and they encourage us to pay attention to the original context of a passage. These questions are necessary if we are to understand how God has been present in the past and what God has done with God's people before us. However, these questions are only the beginning of our work with a passage. When we study the Bible, we also want to bring its stories into conversation with our own life experiences. We need to wonder aloud about a text's relevance to our contemporary concerns. We need to struggle with the cultural differences between the original people and faith communities of the Bible and ourselves. We must work at "translating" ancient teachings into contemporary lessons that honor the spiritual power of the original message and speak to the spiritual needs of our circumstances.

Questions that help us relate the biblical text to our contemporary lives are called "experiential" questions. These are the questions that take us from consideration of what biblical writers such as the author of James mean by "sordidness and rank growth of wickedness" to what "wicked conduct" among Christians looks like in our congregation when we gather to do business. To help us explore the connection between James 1:19–25 and contemporary experience, we might plan such questions as, When do we feel tempted to speak quickly and angrily rather than to listen carefully? What are the temptations faced by contemporary congregations that might interfere with good relationships among members? What parts of church life make us uncomfortable? When has our congregation failed to act in accordance with its own mission statement? What gets in the way of our ability to respond in concrete ways to what we believe is God's will? What practices in our church promote action in response to God's word? All these questions ask us to think about the biblical text in terms of our own context and our personal ideas. They bring the Bible and human experience into conversation with each other.

After we have asked what a text means in its original context and what its relevance is to our own place and time, we need to turn our attention to exploring what response we might make to all we have learned in our engagement with the text. We do this by asking "responsive" questions that prompt us to name feelings and actions called forth by our study. The passage from James might generate these questions: In what ways do we feel empowered by this text to be "doers of the word"? and What practices will we use to encourage careful listening in our congregational gatherings? These questions also guide us into a discussion of the particular agenda item or committee goal to which our Bible study is linked. In the case of James and the behavioral covenant item, we might ask, How well does this proposed behavioral covenant reflect the teachings in James about ideal community life? How will this behavioral covenant help us to rid ourselves of our particular bad habits and become faithful doers of the word?

I have found that my own questions about a text, its relationship to my life, and my response of faith are good guides for the questions I ask others to consider in Bible study. If I am wondering what something means or how it's relevant to today, then I suspect others have similar questions. So I ask these questions aloud for the whole group's benefit. I also ask group members broad questions, such as, What verses or ideas bother you in this text? and What details in this story are unclear after our first reading? This gives others an opportunity to ask questions of clarification about parts of the text that did not generate confusion for me. Then the group can work together to make the confusing areas more clear for everyone. I give some thought ahead of time to how my personal experience relates to the text I have chosen for us to study so that I can offer an example of that connection if group members are struggling to see a relationship. I do the same with regard to my response to the text, although I fully expect that my engagement with the text in a group setting will offer new ideas and energy for that response. If we expect the Bible to act as the living word of God in our midst, then each encounter with the Bible—even those we prepare to lead—has the potential to inform and transform our lives as God's faithful people.

When we decide to study the Bible together as committee members, we must find appropriate passages for study and create a set of questions to guide our exploration. Our study together, however, will be most fruitful if we also cultivate the ability to listen carefully and compassionately to one another as we engage the scriptures. This task can be harder than designing a Bible study, for it requires that we create an environment in which those who are shy are sufficiently comfortable to speak what is on their hearts and minds, and those who are gregarious are sufficiently comfortable with maintaining adequate periods of silence so that others may speak. We contribute to this kind of environment by practicing the basics of good group communication: stating our own thoughts as personal ideas rather than universal claims ("I think" rather than "everybody knows"), paying attention to who has spoken and who has yet to speak, allowing one individual to finish a statement before others begin to speak, and permitting differences of opinion to be shared without fear of condemnation. Sometimes, especially in larger groups with several talkative people, the only way we can make space for quieter persons to speak is to go around the circle or room and offer each person an opportunity in turn. We can also acknowledge the ideas that have already been shared and then specifically invite others to offer ideas that differ from— perhaps even contradict—those expressed. In a particularly quiet group, we can encourage discussion by waiting comfortably in the silences that follow our questions until someone is ready to speak. Those who are shy or reserved often find it easier to break silence than to break into a conversation.

We can also model good listening by attending carefully to what each person in the group says and responding to their ideas, rather than fiddling with our notes or rushing on to the next "point" to be covered. Listening is not as highly valued as speaking in our society, and many of us struggle to be attentive to another's words instead of simply biding time until we can speak ourselves. We tend to act as a collection of individuals, each with her or his own "sound bite" to air for general consumption. Bible study designed to help us discern God's will as a group requires that we function as a true community, formed and shaped by the interaction of various members and their ideas. Active listening—the art of attending carefully and respectfully to another's words—helps transform collectives into communities.

Bible study is only one of the tools that committees can use to invite God to their committee meetings. We might decide to engage instead in worship, silent prayer, or social justice activities as a means of welcoming the divine presence into our deliberations. While the precise skills needed to lead these other activities may differ from those needed for Bible study, the general abilities required remain the same. We still need to identify materials or activities appropriate to our committee work, create a format in which to engage these materials or undertake these actions, and encourage a group process that invites all to participate. In the beginning, this can be difficult work. Our first attempts at small group worship, silent prayer, short Bible studies, or justice-oriented reflection may feel awkward and contrived. That's the norm for first tries. Our first cake was probably rather lopsided, and our first plumbing job may have required additional parts or even outside assistance before the leak was fully repaired. But with perseverance and some resources at hand that model the process for us, I believe that all our committees can gather around meeting tables graced with God's loving and active presence.

And so it is with great excitement about the future vitality of the church that I invite you to explore the specific committee devotional resources in the following chapters. Begin with the chapter that most closely represents the work of your committee, but don't stop there. Many of the resources are useful in multiple settings, for much of our committee work shares the same form and general administrative concerns. Pick your springboard and dive right into the process of inviting God to attend your next board or committee meeting.

Chapter 4

Asking God to Serve on the Church Council/Executive Board

Religious councils have received much bad press in the scriptures and church history. The gospel writers condemned the councils of the chief priests of Jerusalem for their interactions with Jesus and the early church without fully appreciating their important role in conserving Jewish tradition. Church historians have rightly portrayed historic Christian councils such as Chalcedon (in 451 C.E.) and Trent (in 1545 C.E.) as bodies that left the church with a legacy of church doctrine steeped in the blood of those condemned as heretics. However, contemporary Christians have little appreciation for the necessity of these church leaders' engaging in theological debate for the good of the church.

Church councils and executive boards are contemporary local manifestations of these earlier decision-making bodies, and their purposes are to encourage the dynamic conservation of the tradition and to reflect theologically on the truth claims of the church. Their challenge is to undertake these two purposes in such a way that they develop and maintain an appropriate vision for the whole life of the church, rather than degenerating into a body that simply sits in judgment of others' visions, or worse, dispenses altogether with vision as a council concern. Conserving the tradition in a dynamic fashion requires church councils to know the history and practices of the church universal and their own congregation and to imagine how that history and those practices might best be expressed in their particular faith communities. Reflecting theologically on the truth claims of the church requires an ongoing conversation about who God is and what it means to be God's people in a particular time and place.

Faithful executive boards need to take seriously the admonishment of 1 Peter 3:15–16 to the churches of Asia Minor: "Always be ready to make your defense to anyone who demands from you an accounting for the hope that is in you; yet do it with gentleness and reverence." These groups of lay leaders have, in many respects, a daunting task, for they are—with their pastors—the primary spokespeople for God's will in their congregations. The only way in which they can fulfill this role faithfully is if they intentionally seek God's counsel in their council deliberations.

The prophet Jeremiah offers church councils this challenge and promise:

> For who has stood in the council of the LORD
> so as to see and to hear God's word?
>
> I did not send the prophets, yet they ran;
> I did not speak to them, yet they prophesied.
> But if they had stood in my council,
> then they would have proclaimed my words to my
>   people,
> and they would have turned them from their evil way,
> and from the evil of their doings.
>
> (Jer. 23:18, 21–22)

When executive boards stand in God's council, faithfully seeking the ways that God would have them understand the traditions of the church and envision the embodiment of Christian life for their congregations today, then God has promised that all God's people will be transformed by that vision. Serving on the church council is a call to lead God's people in the way they should go, and those who hear this call need to remain attentive to the everlasting counsel of the God who was, and is, and evermore will be.

+ + +

Resource 1   *Seeking a spirit of wisdom and enlightenment*

Church councils and executive boards often must weigh the merits of various proposals related to staffing, programming, funding priorities, building usage, and other administrative concerns of the church. Sometimes these proposals come as recommendations from other committees in the congregation and thus represent the hopes and dreams of that group. They may also arise from an executive board's own revolving calendar of concerns. Dealing with either of these types of proposals can become a perfunctory process of rubber-stamping recommendations or repeating past actions. Encourage a more spiritually energized consideration of your church's administrative business with the following devotion, which contains a Bidding Prayer designed to help participants reflect on the scripture reading and ask for God's guidance.

SCRIPTURE READING: EPHESIANS 1:17–19

> I pray that the God of our Lord Jesus Christ, the Father of glory, may give you a spirit of wisdom and revelation as you come to know him, so that, with the eyes of your heart enlightened, you may know what is the hope to which he has called you, what are the riches of his glorious inheritance among the saints, and what is the immeasurable greatness of his power for us who believe, according to the working of his great power.

BIDDING PRAYER

> Leader: Let us pray to the God of our Lord Jesus Christ, the Father of glory:
>
> Voice 1: May God's Spirit reveal to us God's wisdom, that our eyes might be opened to who God is and our

hearts might be enlightened by that knowledge.
(Silence)

Leader: Spirit of God,
People: **Descend upon our hearts.**
Leader: Let us pray to the God of our Lord Jesus Christ,
the Father of glory:
Voice 2: May God's Spirit enliven us with the hope that
God is actively transforming our world.
(Silence)

Leader: Spirit of God,
People: **Descend upon our hearts.**
Leader: Let us pray to the God of our Lord Jesus Christ,
the Father of glory:
Voice 3: May God's Spirit encourage us to take our places
in divine fellowship with all the saints who have
labored with God through the ages.
(Silence)

Leader: Spirit of God,
People: **Descend upon our hearts.**
Leader: Let us pray to the God of our Lord Jesus Christ,
the Father of glory:
Voice 4: May God's Spirit make known to us the great-
ness of God's power, that we might be compelled
to join in God's saving work in the world.
(Silence)

Leader: Spirit of God,
People: **Descend upon our hearts.**

SUNG RESPONSE: "DAY BY DAY"

Day by day, day by day,
O dear Lord, three things I pray:
To see thee more clearly,
Love thee more dearly,
Follow thee more nearly,
Day by day.

BLESSING
>   Leader: Let us do our work with prayer and praise always
>   in our hearts.
>   People: **Amen.**

Options

Additional petitions that ask God's guidance regarding specific decisions before the group may be added to the bidding prayer, either by continuing the form of the prayer as it is printed or by inviting participants to name concerns aloud following the last petition. (Voice 4 might continue: "Let us name aloud those decisions for which we seek God to compel our actions.") If a group prefers to omit the Sung Response, the Bidding Prayer may be followed by a brief silence and then the Blessing. Groups that prefer more traditional hymnody might substitute "Spirit of God, Descend upon My Heart" (*CH,* 265; *UMH,* 500; *NCH,* 290) for the "Day by Day" chorus.

This short devotion is also an excellent way to begin a congregational or all-church meeting for business.

Resource 2 *Discerning the value of particular programs*

Budget consideration can be one of the most contentious and time-consuming tasks of a church council or executive board. Deciding how to divide the financial pie is often a matter of weighing the anticipated expenses of numerous programs and staff persons against income projections and then determining who gets what for the coming year based on some assessment of which programs are most essential or cost-effective. The norms of the business world tend to prevail in these assessments, and programs that deliver measurable results, such as attendance increases, positive comments from significant members of the congregation, and, most especially, increases in financial contributions, fare well in the budgetary process. Programs with less tangible benefits or little notice are susceptible to budget stagnation or even budget cuts. The following Bible study will help the members of your council or board consider how biblical norms regarding money relate to their budgetary practices.

BIBLE STUDY

Read *Matthew 26:6–13*. Because this is a familiar scripture passage, participants may bring preconceived ideas about what the text means and why it is important. Invite them to think about the text in terms of the assumptions the disciples and Jesus have about what makes something valuable. These three questions may help them explore this issue:

1. How are the disciples measuring the worth of the woman's actions? (One term that might describe their norm is *cost efficiency*.)
2. What measure is Jesus using to determine the value of the woman's actions? (One interpretation is that Jesus focuses on the extent to which the woman's actions testify to God's love and presence, and therefore help people to know God better.)
3. What is the woman's role in the story? (In addition to revealing something about who Jesus is, her actions encourage the disciples to rethink their assumptions about how such actions ought to be evaluated.)

Discuss the ways in which the group's deliberations tend to focus on cost efficiency, and try to identify times when those deliberations focus on the power of a program to reveal God's presence or nurture spirituality. Then ask,

1. How can we consider all the possibilities for how a program or idea contributes to the good of the church?
2. Whom do we need to consult so that we don't become "stuck" in a narrow viewpoint regarding how we value programs and staff persons?

Close with prayer, asking God to help you make good fiscal decisions that take into account the spiritual worth of particular activities and people.

Options

A council or board that wants to transform its budgetary process along the lines of this Bible study might agree to consider carefully at this meeting one program or program area in terms of how it contributes to the good of the church. This discipline, if practiced over several months, would help the group identify key individuals to consult about program worth and develop a discernment practice for their next budgetary cycle.

Resource 3   *Establishing bylaws for God's people*

Many congregations operate with a constitution and by-laws or a book of order and congregational covenant that govern their corporate life. To the church council or executive board falls the task of interpreting these guidelines and occasionally revising them in light of new contexts and congregational concerns. These groups can choose to make such interpretations and revisions only with reference to whether the bylaw in question conforms to conventional organization practices. Or they can consider the components of their congregational covenant in light of the scripture's teachings as well as the wisdom of organizational research. The following Bible study helps focus attention on the spiritual foundations and purposes of organizational rules.

BIBLE STUDY

Read *Deuteronomy 4:5–8* and discuss the following questions:

1. What are the purposes of the "statutes and ordinances" that Moses gives the community?
2. How can we determine if our bylaws (covenant, etc.) accomplish similar purposes?

Read through the congregation's organizational guidelines or have someone highlight the major "rules" of your faith community. Using the criteria generated by your discussion of question 2 (above), consider how well your congregation's "statutes and ordinances" compare with those of the community described in Deuteronomy. If there are significant differences in purpose, you may wish to begin a more thorough process of evaluation and revision. If you feel your congregation's governing principles are consistent with God's expectations for faith communities, you are ready to reflect on a second scriptural passage.

Read *Matthew 22:34–40*. Consider these questions:

1. What "laws" are foundational to Christian life?
2. How can we implement our bylaws (covenant) so that they "hang" on these foundational laws?

Conclude your study with a prayer asking for God's help in implementing your bylaws (covenant) in the specific ways identified in your discussion of the Matthew passage.

Options

This Bible study can be used in two separate meetings if a council or board wishes to explore each passage and its relationship to the congregation's bylaws (covenant) in greater detail. This study might also be used by a subcommittee charged with developing or revising a community's constitution. In this case, shift the language in the second question of each segment, asking, What kind of bylaws would help us accomplish purposes similar to those stated by Moses? and What kind of covenant would grow out of the foundations stated in the Matthew passage? References to these two passages could also be included in written and oral communications about a congregation's bylaws, and a congregation-wide study of these two passages could be part of an annual meeting or all-church covenant discernment process.

Resource 4 *Responding faithfully to congregational conflict*

Rare is the church that carries out its mission without conflict. Different understandings of church life, varying interpretations of congregational priorities, and human sinfulness all contribute to uneasy tensions among members and constituencies. The biblical churches also experienced conflicts, and the accounts of their conflict resolution methods can help contemporary congregations address the inevitable disagreements that mark community life. The following Bible study is designed to help a council or board respond to a congregational conflict with wisdom and compassion.

BIBLE STUDY

Read *Acts 6:1–6,* having one person read the narrative and another read the words of the twelve apostles. Then use the following questions to reflect on the passage's meaning for your situation.

1. What is the nature of the conflict in the Jerusalem church?
2. How does the Jerusalem church deal with this problem?
3. How does faith (spirituality) enter into the church's response?
4. How might this model influence our ways of dealing with congregational concerns in general? in this particular instance?

After discussing ways in which the council or board as a whole might respond to community conflicts, help members personalize the issue by asking them to reflect silently on the question, How can I, as a person of faith and a council (board) member, take responsibility for the health of this congregation's ministries?

Allow two or three minutes for silent reflection, then invite those who wish to share their personal responses with the group. Conclude with a prayer of thanksgiving for scriptural models, and ask God's help in implementing a faithful response to the conflict at hand.

Options

A council or board need not wait until a congregational conflict occurs to engage in this study. Use it during times of congregational harmony to develop a policy and procedures for responding to future conflicts. Or focus more attention on the last question of the study, and use it as an opportunity to reflect on what God requires of each board or council member in his or her role as a steward of the congregation's health and welfare. Rather than sharing individual ideas in a discussion format, the group could gather in a circle for prayer and take turns asking God to help them do something specific that would nurture health in the congregation.

This study also addresses the practice of delegating some leadership responsibilities to other individuals or ad hoc committees appointed by the board or council. If the group wishes to focus on this topic, the following set of questions can be substituted for those given above:

1. What situation prompted the appointment of new leaders?
2. How did the apostles justify their decision to expand the leadership structure of the community?
3. What were the criteria by which new leaders were selected?
4. In what way did these new leaders receive the authority to lead?
5. How might the example of the Jerusalem church help us decide when we need new leaders and who they might be?

The group might then pray together for wisdom in discerning the leadership needs and potential leaders of the congregation.

Resource 5 *Regathering or recovenanting with one another and God*

Many faith communities identify a Sunday (often in the early fall) as a time for recommitting themselves to the church's ministries. Sometimes this is the Sunday on which church school classes reconvene after a summer hiatus and the time of worship returns to its regular hour after a summer schedule. For other traditions, this Sunday coincides with the anniversary of the founding of the congregation or with a prescribed Sunday in the denominational calendar. Some churches plan such Sundays around New Year's Day, borrowing from the cultural calendar's emphasis on new beginnings to focus on their own desire for renewal.

Although these events are often planned by the pastor(s), many clergy would welcome the opportunity to think about and plan for a recovenanting service with the lay leaders of the congregation. Lay participation in discerning the need for and purposes of renewal helps create a climate in which congregations can truly embrace a new sense of God's presence in their midst and recommit themselves to carrying the good news into all the world. A biblical example from the Hebrew Scriptures can facilitate participation by board or council members in the planning process.

BIBLE STUDY

Read *Nehemiah 7:73b—8:3, 9–12.* To emphasize the drama of the text, two people might share the role of narrator, with others taking the roles of Ezra and the Levites. (This can be done informally, with the narrators taking alternate verses and the other voices coming in as needed. Or the group leader can print out a "script" with each part noted separately.) Note that this passage describes an event that occurred in the fifth century B.C.E., following the return of the Israelites from exile in Babylon and the rebuilding of Jerusalem's city walls. Discuss these questions:

1. What is Ezra reading to the people?
2. Who is included in the assembly?
3. Why do you think Ezra and the people are engaged in this activity?
4. Why do you think the people were crying while they listened to the law being read?
5. How do Ezra and the Levites (religious leaders) respond to the people's sadness and grief?
6. Why is rejoicing an appropriate response for the people to make?
7. What aspects of God's plans for our congregation have we forgotten in the last year(s)?
8. What words need to be proclaimed to us so that we might once again rejoice in the fullness of God's salvation and celebrate God's mercy and care?

Use your responses to questions 7 and 8 as a starting point for planning a regathering or recovenanting service that will help your congregation confess the ways it has neglected God's call and rejoice in a new opportunity to do what God would have them to do.

Options

If your group is accustomed to studying the Bible together, you may not need to use the "clarifying" questions (numbers 1, 2, and 5) unless the group is having trouble keeping the central details of the story in mind as it discusses the text experientially (questions 3, 4, and 6) and responsively (questions 7 and 8). If some members of the group are particularly interested in the historical context of the story, the leader might prepare a brief explanation of the situation. Such information can be obtained from a study Bible—look at the introduction to the books of Ezra and Nehemiah—or a Bible commentary. The group also might celebrate with refreshments after the Bible study, just as the Israelites did in the fifth century B.C.E.

In addition to its use in a council or board meeting, this text can be an excellent resource for beginning and ending the actual regathering service. Use the first three verses in a call to worship and verses 9–12 in a commissioning and benediction. One way to shape this would be as follows:

CALL TO WORSHIP

Leader: When the time came—the people of Israel being settled in their towns—all the people gathered together into the square.

People: **They told the scribe Ezra to bring the book of the law of Moses, which the Lord had given to Israel.**

Leader: He read from it from early morning until midday, in the presence of the men and the women and those who could understand,

People: **And the ears of all the people were attentive to the book of the law.**

All: **Amen! Amen!**

COMMISSIONING AND BENEDICTION

Leader: This day is holy to the Lord your God; do not mourn or weep. Go your way, eat the fat and drink sweet wine and send portions of them to those for whom nothing is prepared, for this day is holy to our Lord; and do not be grieved, for the joy of the Lord is your strength, and the Lord's blessing is upon you.

People: **Amen! Amen!**

Resource 6 *Developing a behavioral covenant for life together*

Many congregations assume that all is well with their community until a crisis or conflict threatens to overwhelm or divide them. Then angry and hurtful words are exchanged, leaders are vilified or "dismissed," and some individuals leave the church feeling victimized, while others remain with the same impression. An executive board or church council that recognizes the potential for such "dysfunctional" church family behavior can help prevent it by advocating a behavioral covenant for congregational life. The following Bible study will help council or board members explore possible tenets of such a covenant. A longer exploration of this passage is suggested in chapter 3, where this text is used as an example of how to create a committee Bible study.

BIBLE STUDY

Read *James 1:19–25* aloud two or three times. Use more than one translation so that the ideas expressed in this passage are illumined by different word choices. Looking carefully at each sentence, discuss this question:

1. What actions and attitudes are we asked to avoid? Why?

Make a list of these forbidden activities on newsprint and post it where everyone can see it. Then return to verses 22 and 25 and consider these questions:

2. What action are we asked to take? Why?
3. What is the "word" that we hear and act upon?

Note the group's responses to these questions on another sheet of newsprint and post it next to the first. Then ask:

4. How might a behavioral covenant help us be "doers of the word" (list 2) rather than participants in the harmful actions and attitudes contained in our first list?
5. What are three specific behaviors that describe being "doers of the word"?

Shape your responses to question 5 into three positive statements about how members of your congregation will treat one another. Then try to engage intentionally in these behaviors during your council or board meeting. At the end of the meeting, assess how well you managed to be "doers of the word" with one another.

Options

One effective method of developing an all-church behavioral covenant is to ask each church committee to engage in this study and practice. Then the various committee statements about how we might be "doers of the word" are collected and discussed at a congregational meeting, with additional ideas being solicited from those who were not part of the committee process. When a complete congregational list of ideas has been compiled, the statements can be organized into related groupings, and a small group can be designated to polish the wording and format into a behavioral covenant shared by all who participate in the life of the community. This covenant should be tested by boards and committees through intentional use and assessment over a period of six months to one year. Then the congregation might reconvene to reflect on the ways in which congregational life has been enhanced by the use of the covenant and to modify the covenant as seems appropriate after this trial period.

Resource 7   *Exploring the church's identity*

An important aspect of church life is the organizational management of a congregation's activities. Many churches are rethinking their committee structures as traditional positions go unfilled for lack of volunteers. The church council or executive board can function as the forum for such a reconsideration of how the church organizes its ministries. By looking at the scriptural account of the Jerusalem church's early years, the council or board can imagine ways in which the congregation might define and oversee its work together.

BIBLE STUDY

Read *Acts 2:42–47,* with a different person reading each sentence of the text. (Note: sentences and verse designations do not correspond; do not follow the verse designations. You may wish to print the sentences on a handout that you disseminate to the group.) Ask the group,

1. What are the various activities in which the Jerusalem congregation was engaged? (List these activities on newsprint.) Go back through the list and categorize these activities under four headings:

   Education   Worship   Fellowship   Outreach

Look at a chart or list of your current congregational committees and programs. Ask the group,

2. How might these committees and programs fit into the four emphases of the Jerusalem church structure?
3. In what ways would this simple structure benefit our congregation?
4. If there are committees or programs that do not fit into this structure, what is their purpose in the life of our congregation? Should we continue to engage in these activities? Why or why not?

Use your responses to these questions to affirm or redesign your congregation's organizational structure. Those who decide to redesign their structure might do so for a trial period of one or two years. Throughout this period, members of your congregation could be invited periodically to share their concerns about and appreciation for the trial structure. If the new structure proves effective, then the congregation could make the necessary constitutional or bylaw changes to effect a long-term change.

Options

Councils or boards that do not wish to engage in conversation about structural changes might use this study to think about the multifaceted nature of church life. Rather than imagining how their current congregational organization fits the Jerusalem church model, they might use the experience of identifying the categories of ministry from the Acts passage as a model for sketching out their own congregation's categories. They might consider how these organizational structures help them to attract new members, as verse 47 suggests was true of the Jerusalem church's structure.

Resource 8 *Encouraging congregational leadership development*

Every church, no matter what its organizational structure, depends on congregational leaders to assist it in fulfilling its vision and directing its ministries. Even congregations that place a heavy emphasis on the authority of the pastor and expect him or her to be actively involved as a leader in all aspects of church life also need dependable and capable lay leaders to assist the pastor. Exploring the following scripture passage in a board or council meeting can help current church leaders clarify their reasons for and practices of leadership development.

BIBLE STUDY

Read together *Ephesians 4:7, 11–13.* (In order to do a unison reading, provide all participants with similar Bibles or photocopies of the same version.) Discuss the five leadership roles (apostle, prophet, evangelist, pastor, teacher) given in verse 11. List each role on a separate piece of newsprint mounted on the wall and create a definition or list of attributes that the group would attach to each role. Possible definitions might include

> *Apostle*—one who has a well-rooted relationship with God that permeates his/her entire life and makes him/her a model of faithfulness for others
> *Prophet*—someone who can relate the gospel to contemporary issues and encourages others to respond faithfully to these connections
> *Evangelist*—a person who can tell others about God's love for them in ways that encourage others to desire their own relationships with God
> *Pastor*—one who shares the good news of God's compassion and love by caring for others in need
> *Teacher*—someone capable of encouraging others to study and practice the scriptures, rituals, and traditions of the church with an expectation that they will be transformed

Once the group has agreed on some working definitions or attribute lists, consider who among the group might have one or more of these gifts. Note that persons may show signs of possessing some of these gifts, but the gifts may not yet have been called forth and developed. Then ask,

1. Who else in our congregation appears to have one or more of these gifts?
2. How might we encourage these individuals to develop and use their gifts for the church's benefit?

End your study with a prayer asking God to assist your board or council as you continue to identify and encourage the gifted leaders your congregation needs.

Options

This study can also be refocused to consider the two statements about the purposes of church leadership in verses 12–13. If your board or council prefers this approach, follow this study outline:

Note that Paul contends that Christ has given gifts of leadership so that congregational leaders will

1. *equip the saints for the work of ministry* and
2. *build up the body of Christ.*

Discuss the ways in which your congregation's leaders are expected to help prepare people for the various ministries in which your congregation engages. Then explore how your leaders are expected to nurture the spiritual formation of individuals and the church as a whole. If your congregation has written job descriptions for congregational leaders, look at a few of these job descriptions and ask,

1. How does this description encourage this leader to fulfill the purposes identified by Paul in Ephesians?
2. How might this description need to be redefined to better represent these purposes?

Pray that God will help your council or board nurture effective congregational leaders who faithfully equip and build up your faith community. If appropriate, covenant with one another to assess and revise your congregational job descriptions for leaders so that they better represent the purposes to which you believe leaders are called. Boards and councils of churches that do not already utilize such job descriptions might want to develop such guidelines for their leaders.

Resource 9 *Negotiating between cultural and biblical models of organizational life*

One of the premises of this book is that congregations struggle to discover faithful ways of organizing themselves in the midst of powerful cultural pressures to behave as most other social institutions behave. This is an ancient struggle for God's people, and the tension between cultural norms and biblical norms will remain a part of congregational life until the realm of God is fully realized. Boards and councils that want to intentionally examine this tension within their congregations can use the following Bible study to illumine what is at stake in negotiating an appropriate relationship between God's expectations and cultural practices.

BIBLE STUDY

Read the story of King Josiah of Judea and the prophet Huldah in *2 Kings 22:8—23:3*. This passage contains several unfamiliar biblical names, so select a few confident readers to present it. The text also can be read in parts, with a narrator, King Josiah, high priest Hilkiah, priest's assistant Shaphan, and prophet Huldah speaking in turn. Discuss these questions:

1. What has been discovered in the temple? (Note: The "book of the law" mentioned in verse 8 is most likely an

early form of the book of Deuteronomy, which contains an interpretation of God's covenant with God's people and explains the laws by which God expects people to live.)

2. Why does this discovery upset King Josiah? (Note: Read *Deuteronomy 28:15–28* to get a sense of what King Josiah may have read in the scroll brought to him by Shaphan.)
3. Why does Josiah consult the prophet Huldah?
4. What words of judgment and of hope does Huldah's response contain?
5. What expectations do we think God has for our community of faith?
6. In what ways have we "made offerings to other [cultural] gods" instead of honoring God's expectations?
7. How can we renew our congregational covenant with God?

Join in a litany of covenant renewal to reaffirm your congregation's commitment to honor God's expectations. Use the litany provided below, or fashion your own litany using your group's responses to question 5 as statements of what you are thankful to be doing, your question 6 responses as confessional statements, and your question 7 responses as articulations of the promises you make for the future.

LITANY OF COVENANTAL RENEWAL

Group 1: God, as your people we have tried to be faithful to your expectations.
We have prayed together regularly for your guidance.

Group 2: *We have cared for the needy through our outreach projects. We have tried to teach our children the stories of our faith.*

Group 1: But at times we have failed to be your faithful people.

We have made decisions that have set some
people's gifts above others.

Group 2:   *We have feared and neglected the strangers in
our community. We have been overcome by the
commercialism of our culture.*

Group 1:   Draw us back to you, O God, and teach us
your ways.
We commit ourselves anew to prayer and
study of the scriptures.

Group 2:   *We pledge to investigate the needs of our immediate community and to respond to those needs
with mercy and compassion.*

All: **O God, let our covenant with you be
renewed today!**

Options

This Bible study experience can be enhanced by the creation of specific lists of biblical expectations and cultural practices that are in tension within a particular congregation (e.g.,
regular worship and soccer scheduling, missions giving and
immaculate building maintenance, gifted teachers and vol-
unteerism, etc.). Once a board or council identifies the particular issues that challenge its congregational life, the group can
brainstorm and assess strategies that they might use to help them
manage these issues faithfully.

Resource 10   *Modeling right relationships in God's realm*

Paul often wrote about the importance of right relationships to the churches he founded. Maintaining healthy and
productive relationships with any group of people can be challenging. Add in disagreements about church policies and
procedures, differing viewpoints on the most important aspects
of a church's ministry, and diverse tastes in interior decorating,

and some internal bickering and hurt feelings are bound to occur. Thus, boards and councils may want to remind themselves periodically of the kind of community life God asks of us. A study of a portion of Paul's letter to the Colossians can provide this reminder.

BIBLE STUDY

Ask participants to read *Colossians 3:12–17* silently to themselves. Pause for a minute more of silence to let the words resonate within each person. Then read the passage aloud, using the following responsive form:

RESPONSIVE READING OF COLOSSIANS 3:12–17

> Group 1: As God's chosen ones, holy and beloved, clothe yourselves with compassion, kindness, humility, meekness, and patience.
>
> Group 2: *Bear with one another and, if anyone has a complaint against another, forgive each other;*
>
> Group 1: Just as the Lord has forgiven you, so you also must forgive.
>
> Group 2: *Above all, clothe yourselves with love, which binds everything together in perfect harmony.*
>
> Group 1: And let the peace of Christ rule in your hearts, to which indeed you were called in the one body.
>
> Group 2: *And be thankful.*
>
> Group 1: Let the word of Christ dwell in you richly;
>
> Group 2: *Teach and admonish one another in all wisdom;*
>
> Group 1: And with gratitude in your hearts sing psalms, hymns, and spiritual songs to God.
>
> Group 2: *And whatever you do, in word or deed, do everything in the name of the Lord Jesus, giving thanks to God the Father through him.*

Ask participants to identify the phrases from the reading that resonated most powerfully within them during their two readings of the passage. Explore the reasons for their choices by asking, Why do you think this phrase stood out to you today?

Conclude your discussion by asking participants to pray together, each giving thanks (silently or aloud) for the ways in which your congregation exemplifies the Colossians model or requesting God's help in living up to some aspect of the model that is eluding your congregation at this time.

Options

Boards and councils whose congregations are embroiled in controversies might extend this study to include a specific assessment of their congregational practices according to norms advocated by Paul. Write each section of the responsive reading at the top of a separate sheet of newsprint, and then work as a whole or in small groups to identify ways in which your congregation exemplifies and/or falls short of each norm for faithful community life. An innovative method for accomplishing this task is to give each participant a sticky note pad and have people write comments on sheets from the pads, posting them on the appropriate sheet of newsprint. Once the lists are compiled, review the lists together, affirming and celebrating those things your congregation does well and brainstorming methods to improve those practices with which your congregation struggles.

Chapter 5

Asking God to Serve on the Christian Education Committee

In both the Old and the New Testaments, Christian education is cited as a central aspect of the life of the faith community. In Psalm 78 the psalmist demands that God's people "give ear" to the psalmist's teachings; the people reply, "We will tell to the coming generation the glorious deeds of the LORD, and God's might, and the wonders that God has done." In Acts 2:42, the members of the early church "devoted themselves to the apostles' teaching." The purpose of the Christian education committee, then, is to encourage the teaching of God's word and to foster a safe, inviting atmosphere in which people can study the scriptures and "try on" Christian identity. This board probes the educational concerns of the congregation and engages children, youth, and adults in reflections on their spiritual journeys and spiritual longings. It reminds the congregation of the value of traditional church teachings and practice while helping the congregation find ways to make the old story relevant to the contemporary world.

The Christian education committee attends to the spiritual longing within all people for a more meaningful life than the one portrayed in our media. It advocates the fundamental theological belief that all people desire to love and be loved by God. It develops programs that cultivate within individuals and groups this desire to be in loving relationship with God and points out God's desire to satisfy this longing. It struggles to sort out with the congregation the proper balance between meeting people where they are and proclaiming the good news that they have come to hear. And it assesses its educational offerings according to its vision of God and people in a mutual, loving, and life-giving relationship.

+ + +

Resource 1 *God's provision of strength in times of weariness*

Perhaps the most exhausting task of the Christian education board is the creation and maintenance of an effective children's church school program. The logistical and recruitment efforts required to collect supplies, staff classes, prepare snacks or special materials, oversee the nursery, and coordinate the movement of many young, energetic bodies to the right place at the right time is immense. Committee members can get tired just thinking about all the details, even if they are good at delegating responsibility. Add to this the fact that such committees often are made up of parents with young children, and weariness becomes an inevitable concern. Acknowledge this reality of the committee's life by beginning your meeting with this devotion:

PRAYER OF INVOCATION

> Leader: God who soars on the wings of wind,
> People: **float gently down to me.**
> Leader: Spirit who rushes on high in the clouds,
> People: **descend powerfully into me.**
> Leader: Christ who rose from death to life,
> People: **raise new life within me.**
> All: **Amen.**

SCRIPTURE READING: ISAIAH 40:21–31

HYMN: "Kum ba yah"
Kum ba yah, my Lord, kum ba yah (*3 times*)
O Lord, kum ba yah.

Someone's weary, Lord...
Come by here, my Lord...

Options

This devotion can be extended to include a study of the Isaiah passage. Questions for discussion might include,

1. How is God portrayed in the reading?
2. What is God's relationship with those who consider themselves powerful?
3. How does God relate to those who are weak and weary?
4. How has God sustained you during the past week (or today)?

If the group is uncomfortable singing together, a spoken prayer requesting God's strengthening presence can be substituted. Or the group might share specific prayer concerns and ask God to renew their strength by bearing those burdens.

Resource 2 *Making plans and trusting God*

The Christian education committee is a working part of the administration of the church. It is also a group of people who come together with personal needs and expectations. As a group, it needs to develop a cohesiveness around a shared vision. As a collection of individuals, it needs to attend to the experiences and contributions of each individual member. The following Bible study and exercise is designed to facilitate a discussion of individual and group goals. It is a particularly useful resource for the first meeting of a new program year.

EXERCISE

Give each group member three sheets of legal sized paper. Then ask them to take one sheet of paper and write (with marker in large print) a word or phrase to complete the following statement:

- The Christian education committee will be successful if we achieve…

Once they have each responded to the first statement, ask the participants to complete this statement on another piece of paper:

- We can do this best by…

When they finish the second statement, invite them to respond to this statement on their third sheet of paper:

- I'll feel good about being a part of the Christian education committee if I…

Collect the first set of answers and post them in a column on the wall, reading them aloud as you go. Label this first column "Goals." Make another column, labeled "Processes," with the second set of answers, and then a third column, labeled "Contributions," with the third set. Reflect with the group on the similarities and differences among various people's responses.

BIBLE STUDY

Read *Mark 4:26–32.* Reflect on how the individual *contributions* the group has listed are like the seeds in these parables, *processes* are like planting, and *goals* are maturation and harvest. Consider these questions:

1. What do these parables tell you about the value of each person's contributions?
2. How do your processes fit with God's ways of working in the world?
3. Who is ultimately responsible for the meeting of your goals?

Options

You can reverse the order of the exercise and Bible study by phrasing the Bible study questions more generally:

1. What seeds (no matter how small) would we like to plant this year?

2. What kinds of expectations can we have about the outcome of our planting?
3. Who brings the harvest?

Use your answers to these questions to shape your responses to the exercise. At the end of the Christian education program year, you can revisit this exercise and Bible study by reflecting on the ways in which the seeds you planted (*contributions*) have come to fruition (*goals*) and how that has happened (*processes*).

Resource 3 *Telling the tradition's stories to new generations*

A major aspect of Christian education is teaching Bible stories and church traditions to children. Curriculum assessment and selection, teacher training and evaluation, and the administration of a children's church school program often occupy the bulk of the board's time. This Bible study focuses the committee's attention on the biblical reasons for engaging in these tasks. It also highlights the important connection between adult Bible study and the teaching of children.

BIBLE STUDY

Read *Psalm 78*. Note that there are two "calls" in this psalm. In verse 1, the psalmist calls on people of faith to listen to the stories. The stated assumption is that people must hear the stories themselves before they can pass them along to the next generation. The second "call" is to teach the stories to the community's children. Several purposes for teaching children are given in verses 6–8. Discuss these questions:

1. What are the reasons the psalmist gives for teaching our children the stories of our tradition?
2. What place do stories that contain "warnings" or "punishment" themes have in our program?
3. What kinds of preparation do we need in order to teach such stories?

Pray that God will guide the committee in finding appropriate ways to help remember and teach the stories of our faith to our children.

Options

The group might also chose to rewrite this psalm as a litany or prayer that could be used during a teacher dedication service. Or each member might name or recount a favorite Bible story and state how that story has helped him or her remain hopeful and faithful to God. An artistic board might make posters highlighting verse 4, which could be posted on a Christian education bulletin board or in church school classrooms.

Resource 4 *Meeting challenges with faithfulness*

As the Christian education board plans and implements its ministries, it will face times when others disagree with its plans or challenge its commitments. The committee may even have to respond to criticism directed toward an individual church school teacher or program director. This Bible study is designed to help the committee discern an appropriate response to such challenges. It encourages board members to think about their reasons for planning certain events and calling particular individuals as educational leaders. It also establishes a framework for assessing the effectiveness of ministries that others question.

BIBLE STUDY

Read *Acts 5:27–42*. In order to understand the event described in the passage, discuss the following questions:

1. What motivates Peter and the apostles in their work?
2. What criterion for assessment does Gamaliel establish?
3. How do the apostles respond in the face of adversity?

Then apply the text to the committee's understanding of its own work and the particular program, person, or goal being questioned. These questions will help the committee move from exegesis (careful reading and interpretation of the text in its context) to application of the text in the contemporary situation:

1. What motivates our work?
2. How can we determine if our goals and plans are God's goals and plans?
3. Are there ways in which this goal, plan, or person is showing signs of failure?
4. How, then, should we respond to criticism and skepticism in this case?

Conclude the Bible study with a prayer praising God for the opportunity to reassess the committee's goals and to move forward with the assurance that the committee is acting in accordance with God's will.

Options

In the absence of specific complaints or concerns, committee members may want to use this Bible study as a springboard for developing criteria by which they will assess the effectiveness of their educational ministries and leaders. Questions 3 and 4 would then be recast as general queries, such as, How will we decide if a program has failed or is energized by God's spirit? and How will we respond to criticism of programs we believe are appropriate and effective?

Resource 5 *Educating all God's people*

Christian education committees often struggle to define themselves as more than the administrators of children's church school classes. This struggle can arise because board members feel too overwhelmed to do anything more than manage the myriad details of organizing children's classes, or because congregations encourage nothing more than a church school focus. For the committee that wants to broaden its understanding of educational ministry, the following Bible study will be helpful.

BIBLE STUDY

Read aloud *Deuteronomy 31:12–13* from three or four different versions of scripture, such as the *New Revised Standard,* the *Contemporary English,* the *King James,* and the *New International* versions. Then consider these questions:

1. Who is included in the educational process in this text?
2. What are the goals of the process? (Note and discuss the different words that describe these goals used by the various Bible versions.)
3. How does our committee and congregation share these goals?
4. What are our concerns about our congregation's educational ministry?

Pray together about your concerns, and ask God's guidance in responding to those concerns during your meeting and in the coming months.

Options

This short biblical passage is also an excellent choice for use in worship on the first Sunday of a new program year. Committee members might create a Call to Worship, borrowing the words or theme of these verses, and also ask the pastor to incorporate this theme in the prayers of the morning. Or these verses might become part of a teacher dedication liturgy, serving to explain the purpose of their calling as Christian educators in the congregation.

Resource 6   *God as the one who teaches us*

Often, members of the Christian education board are also teachers of church school classes. As such, they feel responsible for knowing what it is that God would have them teach, and they may struggle with feelings of inadequacy. They need to be reminded that God will support them in their efforts if only they will turn to God for assistance. The following litany and sung prayer will help everyone on the committee acknowledge the need to be supported and taught by God.

RESPONSIVE READING (based on Jeremiah 32 and Psalm 143)

> Leader: Ah Lord God! It is you who made the heavens and the earth by your great power and by your outstretched arm!
>
> People: **Nothing is too hard for you. You show steadfast love to the thousandth generation.**
>
> Leader: O great and mighty God whose name is the Lord of hosts,
>
> People: **You are great in counsel and mighty in deed, and your eyes are open to all the ways of mortals.**
>
> Leader: Hear my prayer, O Lord;
>
> People: **Answer me in your righteousness.**
>
> Leader: I remember the days of old; I think about all your deeds; I meditate on the works of your hands.
>
> People: **I stretch out my hands to you; my soul thirsts for you like a parched land.**
>
> Leader: Answer me quickly, O Lord; my spirit fails.
>
> People: **Let me hear of your steadfast love, for in you I put my trust.**
>
> Leader: Teach me the way I should go, for to you I lift up my soul.
>
> People: **Teach me to do your will, for you are my God.**

SUNG PRAYER: "SPIRIT OF THE LIVING GOD"

> Spirit of the Living God, fall afresh on me.
> Spirit of the Living God, fall afresh on me.
> Melt me, mold me, fill me, use me.
> Spirit of the Living God, fall afresh on me.

Following the singing of the prayer, invite people to sit quietly in the presence of God's spirit. Close this time of silence with a brief prayer of gratitude for God's teaching in the past and God's willingness to continue teaching us throughout our lives.

Options

Groups that enjoy singing traditional hymns might wish to substitute "Sweet Hour of Prayer" (*CH,*570; *UMH,* 496; *NCH,* 505) for the sung prayer. This hymn would then serve as a call to prayer, and committee members would be invited to share their concerns and petitions after the singing. Committees that are uncomfortable singing could follow the litany with a Bidding Prayer, in which each person states something he or she would like God to teach them, and after each petition the group responds, "We await your teaching, God."

This resource is also useful as a tool for reminding a board to seek God's direction in making decisions about programming, staffing, or expenditures. If a committee has been discussing an issue about which there is disagreement, pausing during the deliberations to remember and seek God's counsel can keep the conversation from degenerating into a battle between committee members' opinions.

Resource 7   *The biblical story and spirituality*

Many adults in our congregations distinguish between "spirituality" and "religion." They may believe that personal participation in spiritual practices like prayer and meditation will bring them inner peace and greater happiness, while at the same time they feel skeptical about the importance of more institutionally-based practices such as Bible study and worship. Such skepticism may be expressed in "soft" terms—statements like "I feel closer to God while walking in the woods than I do in church"—or in more explicit language—"I don't need to read the Bible to be a good person; besides, the Bible is full of stories nobody in their right mind would take seriously!" Adults who grew up in the church often feel that they put in their church school time as children and have now "graduated" from that aspect of religious life. Adults new to church participation may be "too busy" to engage in studies that seem irrelevant to their spiritual perspective.

Christian education boards and committees thus face the challenge of promoting adult education as an essential aspect of spiritual life, rather than simply another programmatic option offered by the church. The following resource will help board or committee members clarify the relationship between Bible study and spirituality for themselves so that they might share a new perspective with the other adults in their congregation.

INTRODUCTION

Ask participants to listen silently to the poem "Is Love" by Maya Angelou. Tell them that the reading will be followed by a minute of silence for reflection.

Midwives and winding sheets
know birthing is hard
and dying is mean
and living's a trail in between.

Why do we journey, muttering
like rumors among the stars?
Is a dimension lost?
Is it love?[1]

Ask participants to share what this poem says to them about spiritual longing. After discussing their experiences of the poem, note that many adults see themselves as spiritual "seekers," looking for meaning and purpose in life. Suggest that Bible study can be a resource for addressing the questions Angelou and many of us pose about life.

BIBLE STUDY

Read *1 Corinthians 1:4–6* aloud and discuss the following questions:

---

[1]Maya Angelou, *The Complete Collected Poems of Maya Angelou* (New York: Random House, 1994), 228.

1. How are the people of Corinth being enriched in their spiritual lives?
2. Where do we find the "testimony [teachings and example] of Christ" today?
3. How is knowledge of Christ's testimony linked to spirituality?
4. What spiritual gifts can you imagine being developed through Bible study?
5. What is the purpose of a spiritual life based on Christ's testimony?

Use your answers to these questions to help you think about how other adults might be drawn into Bible study that develops their spiritual gifts and prepares them to live "blameless" lives of substance rather than "aimless" lives of regret. Pray that God will help you identify adults in your congregation or community who would welcome the good news that God wants to strengthen them in their spiritual sojourn through the testimony of Christ as found in the scriptures.

Options

Instead of beginning with Maya Angelou's poem, the group could begin by sharing their own ideas about why Bible study is or is not important for adults before turning to a scriptural perspective on the issue. Or the group could explore the words of the hymn "Tell Me the Stories of Jesus" (*CH*,190; *UMH*, 277), discuss the ways in which they might affirm or challenge the hymn writer's ideas about the usefulness of studying the scriptures, and then compare the hymn's message with the ideas expressed by Paul in his letter to the Corinthians. This hymn or another on a similar theme also could be used in closing.

Resource 8 *The purpose of religious knowledge*

Biblical literacy is an issue of concern in contemporary congregations. Many children, youth, and adults have little acquaintance with the primary figures and biblical stories once assumed to be commonly held narratives. In response to this lack of basic knowledge, Christian education boards may be tempted to encourage those who teach to focus on Bible "facts" and student comprehension of these "facts." Such an approach, however, loses sight of the primary purpose of religious knowledge as being information that helps people discover ways in which they might live faithfully. Remind your committee of this purpose with a short Bible study taken from the Hebrew Scriptures.

BIBLE STUDY

Read *1 Kings 3:5–9*. End your reading with the words "Here ends our reading from the scripture. May God bless us with understanding." Then wonder together about the following questions:

1. Why does God give Solomon the opportunity to ask for something?
2. What does Solomon want most of all?
3. Why does Solomon make the request that he makes?
4. How have the stories of his own father's relationship with God shaped Solomon's perspective?
5. How has our own biblical knowledge shaped our sense of what God would have us do?
6. How might additional knowledge promote in us "understanding minds," and how might such knowledge get in the way of discernment? (Note: Think about the ways that all kinds of knowledge can be both helpful and harmful. One example of a harmful effect of knowledge is when our reliance on what we know keeps us from seeing new possibilities for relationships or situations.)

Ask each person to think about her or his most recent experience of an educational program and to share the ways in which that experience either promoted or hindered the development of an understanding mind. Conclude your sharing time with a prayer that God will work through the educational ministries of your congregation to cultivate minds capable of discerning leadership.

Options

In verse 15 we learn that this exchange between God and Solomon occurred in a dream. This suggests that religious knowledge can come to us unconsciously (through dreams and visions) as well as through our conscious acquisition of information. Extend this study by exploring the value you place on these and other ways of acquiring religious knowledge. Useful questions for this discussion include

1. With which ways of acquiring religious knowledge are you most comfortable? Why?
2. What methods of acquiring such knowledge make you uncomfortable? Why?

Use your responses to these questions to think about the kinds of knowledge acquisition you encourage in your educational ministries and whether these methods are sufficient to help persons desire and obtain understanding minds.

Resource 9 *Interpreting faithfulness among those we educate*

One of the challenges for those who guide the educational ministries of a congregation is assessing the effectiveness of those ministries. One method of assessment is to measure numeric participation, either in terms of actual numbers or in terms of the percentage of church school participants to church members. Such accountings can be useful for determining programmatic appeal, but they shed little light on the ability of an educational event or set of programs to form persons in faith. To measure the formative power of their educational ministries, Christian education committees need to look at the ways in which members of their congregations are living faithful lives. They need to have a vision of faithful living that they can use as a measure. Paul's letter to the Romans can provide one such norm.

BIBLE STUDY

Read aloud *Romans 12:1–8* from two or three different translations. You might read through the passage entirely more than once or read each segment (verses 1–2, 3–5, 6–8) in more than one translation before moving to the next segment. Using the differences among the translations to help you discern the meaning of the text, explore the following questions:

1. What is Paul saying about being faithful in verses 1–2?
2. What attitudes toward ourselves and others does Paul advocate in verses 3–5?
3. What gifts are church members called in verses 6–8 to use faithfully?
4. How can we measure faithfulness according to this passage?

When you have finished exploring the scripture passage, read aloud the following excerpt from Anne Lamott's book *Traveling Mercies*. Introduce the passage by telling the group that it comes from a chapter in the book titled "Why I Make Sam Go to Church." Sam is Lamott's son, and, as for many kids, church is not his first choice for an activity. But Lamott makes him go anyway, and this passage summarizes her reasons for doing so.

> The main reason [I make Sam go to church] is that I want to give him what I found in the world, which is to say a path and a little light to see by. Most of the people I know who have what I want—which is to say, purpose, heart, balance, gratitude, joy—are people with a deep sense of spirituality. They are people in community, who pray, or practice their faith; they are Buddhists,

Jews, Christians—people banding together to work on themselves and for human rights. They follow a brighter light than the glimmer of their own candle; they are part of something beautiful.[2]

With Lamott's words and the Romans passage in mind, invite participants to share their personal reasons for being part of a religious community. Then discuss these questions:

1. What gifts and orientations toward life do you expect your educational ministries to foster? Make a list of those "faithful living" criteria on which the group agrees.
2. How well do you see these gifts and orientations being lived out in your faith community?

Pray that God will guide you as you continue to use this set of "faithful living" criteria to measure the effectiveness of your educational ministries.

Options

To shorten this study, omit the reading from Lamott and add the questions following that reading to the Bible study. A committee or board might also begin with the Lamott reading and then explore the ways in which the Romans passage offers a specific way of understanding Lamott's more general categories of "purpose, heart, balance, gratitude, joy." The Romans passage need not be viewed as an exhaustive interpretation of these concepts, nor must Lamott's categories be understood as all-inclusive or necessarily biblical. But by laying these two passages side by side, we enter into a conversation about interpreting faithfulness that more easily values both contemporary human experience and traditional biblical testimony.

---

[2]Anne Lamott, *Traveling Mercies: Some Thoughts on Faith* (New York: Random House, 1999), 100.

Resource 10 *Identifying threats to faithfulness and nurturing wise choices*

Many parents bring their children to church because they want help with instilling moral values in their offspring. And many older adults hold the Christian education board or committee responsible for "inappropriate" behavior by children during any church event. Thus, boards and committees can— rightly or wrongly—become the focus of negative attention if the congregation's children do not seem to be living according to the moral or behavioral standards their parents and other adults desire. In addition to educating the congregation about typical stages of child development and reminding other adults of their joint role in forming children in faith, a board or committee can clarify its own sense of appropriate and inappropriate behavior with this study contrasting the "works of the flesh" with the "fruit of the Spirit."

DEFINING THE PROBLEM

Post two sheets of newsprint on the wall. On one sheet, list children's behaviors about which adults in your congregation complain. On a second sheet, list behaviors that the people in your congregation would like to see in children. Leave these lists posted while you engage in the following Bible study.

BIBLE STUDY

Read *Galatians 5:19–23* from both the *New Revised Standard Version* of the Bible and the *Contemporary English Version* Bible (or a similar dynamic translation). Add two more sheets of newsprint to the wall, one next to each of the sheets already posted. On the sheet next to the list of behavioral complaints, write down all the "works of the flesh" condemned by Paul, translating his terms as best you are able into similar behaviors in which children or youth might engage. (For instance, "idolatry" might translate into "having the gimmies" and fornication might be rendered as "making derogatory sexual comments.") Compare your congregation's complaints with those behaviors condemned by Paul. How are the two lists similar? In what ways, if any, are they significantly different?

Then write down the "fruit of the Spirit" next to the list of behaviors adults compliment in children. Compare these two lists using the same questions as before. Then ask yourselves,

1. How serious are our concerns about our children's behavior compared with the concerns Paul had about the Galatians?
2. In what ways are our children already exhibiting the "fruit of the Spirit"?
3. How might we reshape our expectations so that our attention is focused on the kind of life or death issues about which Paul writes?
4. How might we encourage our children to avoid behaviors that Paul calls the "works of the flesh" and choose instead behaviors that exhibit the "fruit of the Spirit"? (Be specific.)

Pray for the children in your congregation and their ongoing formation in faith. Share the fruits of your discussion with other adults in the congregation through a newsletter article or bulletin board display that highlights threats to our children's faithfulness and suggests ways to nurture their wise decision making.

Options

If your board or committee finds it too difficult to translate some of Paul's concerns into terms for children, simply work with those behaviors you can translate and ignore the rest. Similarly, if your group finds the "fruit of the Spirit" concepts too abstract to be useful when thinking about particular age groups of children, then imagine more concrete expressions of this "fruit" and use your ideas for comparative purposes. The point of this study is to focus attention on the struggle between behaviors that are life-giving and those that threaten children's well-being. Just as Paul allowed his cultural context and intended adult audience to affect his choice of behaviors and words, let your own context help set the tone of your conversation.

This study also works well as part of an adult education class on Christian parenting. Your committee might pair this resource with resource 3 in this chapter for an hour-long conversation about the relationship between biblical literacy and moral development in children.

Chapter 6

Asking God to Serve on the Mission, Outreach, and Social Action Committees

The biblical book of James contends with the tensions that often exist between the rich and the poor. Struggling to combat the partiality for the rich and socially well-established that he witnessed in the early church, the author came to the conclusion that faith and works must be inextricably linked in the lives of Christians. He declared, "For just as the body without the spirit is dead, so faith without works is also dead" (Jas. 2:26). It is the task of a congregation's mission, outreach, or social action committee to interpret how its particular Christian community will express its faith through its works of justice and compassion.

That this board goes by many names expresses, in part, the variety of ways in which churches understand God's expectation that they will put their faith to work. Some congregations focus their efforts toward communicating the gospel directly through evangelism coupled with compassionate aid and education. Others take an "actions speak louder than words" approach, offering humanitarian assistance in the name of the church but without articulating an explicitly religious motivation for their actions. Still others seek to affect political and social policy through congregational letter campaigns and participation in public events. Many churches have experienced tense battles around the issue of what constitutes an appropriate mission, outreach, or social action project. Nervous about conflict, some of these churches simply designate a certain amount of money that they will donate to "good causes" during the year and then write checks to the organizations they've "always" supported.

The primary goals of any mission, outreach, or social action committee should be the development of a congregational vision of the relationship between faith and action and the provision of opportunities for church members to participate in the realization of that vision. The congregation's vision is best if it is a contextual one, founded in scripture and framed by the community that surrounds and extends from the church's walls. This means that mission, outreach, and social action boards play a crucial role in investigating the social context and interpreting that context and its needs to congregations. They also become an important means for church members to demonstrate their faith by their works, as the book of James claims we must.

+ + +

Resource 1 *The relationship between true worship and social action*

Many Christians understand Sunday morning worship as the centerpiece of their religious lives, and some see no need for any other religious activities. Participation in mission, outreach, or social action projects may seem like an expendable activity, something they do if they have time or inclination. For this reason, mission, outreach, and social action committees may struggle to generate enough interest in their projects or even cease to offer hands-on opportunities for service in the community and the world. The Hebrew Scriptures' prophets faced this same dilemma in their days, and some of them directly challenged this assumption. Use the words of the prophet Amos to explore this issue in your board meeting.

INTRODUCTION

Ask participants to name the things that they consider to be the most important activities of a Christian life. List these things on newsprint where everyone can see them. As a group, quickly rank the top five items on your list, with one being most important, two being second-most important, and so forth. If you have difficulty agreeing on a ranking for your items, take a few minutes to determine the reasons for your disagreement and either leave the items unranked or give multiple rankings.

BIBLE STUDY

Read *Amos 5:21–24*. Note that Amos was a prophet in Israel during the eighth century B.C.E., when the nation was prosperous and peaceful. His words were falling on the ears of a complacent people happy with their status and achievements. Discuss the following questions:

1. Who is speaking in these verses?
2. Why is God unsatisfied with the people's worship?
3. How does God relate worship, justice, and righteousness to one another?
4. What relationship do worship, justice, and righteousness have to one another in our congregation?

Look back at the list of important Christian activities that you created at the beginning of this study. Discuss how your items and their rankings relate to Amos' teaching. If appropriate, decide together on a new ranking that reflects changes in the group's thinking after exploring the scripture passage. If the group was unable to rank the list on the first try, compare the reasons for your disagreement with the conflict between God and God's people revealed in Amos. See if your study of Amos has helped you come to a consensus about an appropriate ranking.

Pray that your congregation might please God by engaging in both worship- and justice-oriented activities.

Options

The last sentence of this passage (v. 24) is often used as a theme for mission, outreach, and social action events. Jane Parker Huber uses this verse and others from Amos in the hymn "Let Justice Flow Like Streams" (*NCH,* 588). Your committee might sing this short hymn, which is set to a familiar tune, as its closing prayer.

Boards willing to commit only a very short time to study and reflection may omit the exercises involving the creation and review of the Christian activities list. Engagement with the biblical text and the numbered discussion questions, followed by prayer, is sufficient to identify the theme and invite God's perspective into the committee's work. The longer study is designed to help committee members identify and assess their own and the group's perspectives in relation to the text.

Resource 2 *What God requires of us*

This resource shares a similar concern to that of Resource 1: What does God expect from God's people in terms of their engagement in worship and service? Mission, outreach, and social action committees will find themselves asking this question over and over again as they work with church members who are struggling to live faithfully amid competing opportunities for church participation and social activities. Board members themselves may feel stretched thin by their commitments and struggle to provide visionary leadership when what they most desire is to be done with yet another meeting and go home to bed. The purpose of this resource is to help committee members develop a framework for their goals that assists them in persuading others to participate in a life of service pleasing to God and attentive to the demands of contemporary life.

BIBLE STUDY

Read *Micah 6:6–8* responsively in the following manner:

Group 1:   With what shall I come before the LORD,
           and bow myself before God on high?
Group 2:   Shall I come before him with burnt offerings,
           with calves a year old?
Group 1:   Will the Lord be pleased with thousands of
           rams, with ten thousands of rivers of oil?
Group 2:   Shall I give my firstborn for my transgression,
           the fruit of my body for the sin of my soul?
    All: **God has told you, O mortal, what is good;**
           and what does the LORD require of you
           but to do justice, and to love kindness,
           and to walk humbly with your God?

Note that Micah was a prophet in Judah during the eighth and seventh centuries B.C.E., the period when the Assyrians conquered Syria, Israel, and eventually Judah itself. The first two verses of this passage suggest several ways that the people of Judah might have renewed their relationship with God during those troubled times. Verse 8 states what Micah believed were God's expectations for the renewal of the divine-human relationship. Use the following questions to explore the various means suggested for creating a right relationship between God and God's people.

1. Where do you think the various ideas expressed in verses 6 and 7 came from? (Think about the stories of Israelite worship you know and the stories of religious rituals such as human sacrifice that were practiced by many ancient civilizations.)
2. Why do you think the people thought these practices might be what God wanted? (Assume that the people of Judah have some awareness of their own tradition and of other religions and religious practices.)
3. How does Micah's response change the direction of the people's thinking?

4. What does it mean to "do justice"?
5. What does it mean to "love kindness"?
6. What does it mean to "walk humbly with your God"?
7. Why do you think Micah includes all three requirements in his statement about God's expectations?
8. How can our committee (board) help church members meet each of these requirements?

End this study by singing "What Does the Lord Require of You?" (*CH,* 659; *UMH,* 441) and offering to God a brief prayer of thanksgiving for God's guidance.

Options

Mission, outreach, and social action committees who have certain set activities or foci might review those things to see how they fall into the categories offered by Micah. These boards would then have a better idea of their effectiveness in encouraging church members to engage in one or more of these categories. Committees without such a legacy might use the three requirements as a template for developing a range of activities that individually emphasize a single requirement and collectively represent the fullness of God's expectations. (Boards also might apply the template differently, using it to create opportunities that address all three requirements at once.)

This study also could be used to promote conversation about overlapping interests between committee members and those responsible for the worship life of the congregation.

Resource 3 *The need for mission visionaries and leaders*

One of the best ways to help others get involved in Christian service is to provide models of Christian servanthood. Within all our churches there are individuals who share their gifts and abilities with the congregation and the wider community. Sometimes a misplaced emphasis on humility means that very few people know about or value the work being done. Even our acknowledgments of a person's mission or outreach efforts may fail to convey the importance of this work for the life and health of the congregation. If your board or committee is trying to figure out how to motivate new participants in outreach activities and how to keep the ones it has, it needs to consider the congregation's need for mission visionaries to lead the way.

BIBLE STUDY

Read *Acts 9:36–42*. The group may be tempted to focus its attention on the question of whether Dorcas (Tabitha) was really raised from the dead; if so, suggest that the issue of resurrection is an interesting one, but it is not the most helpful way of approaching the text for the committee's purposes. Encourage participants to consider how this passage relates to mission, outreach, and social action concerns by exploring these questions:

1. What is Dorcas known for in her community?
2. How do the other disciples justify their request that Peter try to do something about Dorcas' death?
3. Why do you think Dorcas' community felt so strongly that they needed her presence among them?
4. Who are the witnesses to "good works and acts of charity" in our congregation?
5. How might we lift them up and acknowledge their importance so that others might follow in their stead?

Pray for the mission visionaries you have identified, and ask God to help you reinforce their witness in your congregation.

Options

Committees that are dramatically inclined could act out this passage or invite others to help them present the text in the form of a congregational drama. One way to reinforce the connection between the story of Dorcas and a congregation's own mission visionaries would be to ask a church member who regularly engages in outreach activities to play the role of Dorcas.

The roles of the other disciples might be played by committee members, and the role of Peter might be embodied by a pastor or elder. Committee members would work together to identify symbols of the mission visionary's work and to decide on the verbal arguments they will use to get "Peter" to respond to their need for a miracle.

Once a board has developed this personalized drama, it can use the drama, the identified symbols, and the rationales for valuing mission visionaries as part of its attempts to encourage participation in the mission, outreach, and social action ministries of the congregation.

Resource 4 *God's love for the city*

The problems of inner-city life are well known to most of us, whether we are city dwellers, suburbanites, or rural people. Newspaper accounts of crime and violence often focus on the city, giving the impression that the city is evil, even though statistically, many cities have lower crime rates than other types of communities. Poverty, racism, indifference, and urban decline do indeed breed crime and violence on city streets and in city schools, but our widespread fear of the city and those who live within its poorer neighborhoods can get in the way of our willingness to serve the urban poor.

As Christians, we need to rethink our attitudes toward the city and its residents. Mission, outreach, and social action committees can begin this process by asking themselves how Jesus viewed the city.

INTRODUCTION

Ask participants to share what images and descriptive words come to mind when you say the word "city." Then suggest that the group invite one more voice into the conversation by looking at a scripture passage in which Jesus speaks about the city of Jerusalem.

BIBLE STUDY

Ask someone to read aloud *Luke 19:41–44*. As a group, consider the following questions:

1. How does Jesus *feel* about the city of Jerusalem?
2. What is his specific concern about the city's future?
3. Why does he believe the city will be destroyed?
4. What is needed to prevent the city's destruction?
5. What is destroying our city or the cities we know?
6. What might our congregation do to help prevent the destruction of our city or other cities?

Pray that God might help your congregation feel a genuine concern for the urban poor that motivates your community to engage in city ministry.

Options

If some participants raise questions about the safety of ministry within and to cities, brainstorm concrete ways that your congregation might reach out to the city indirectly while you continue to study and learn about the realities of city life and the possibilities of more "hands-on" forms of ministry. If your congregation is far removed from city life, discuss how you can support urban ministries in a city that is frequently mentioned in your newspaper or that is the focus of your denomination's outreach ministries.

Resource 5   *The healing of the nations*

Every congregation should pay attention to the need for justice and compassionate care in their own communities. Likewise, every congregation needs to consider how its relative wealth in comparison to the rest of the world's resources requires it to seek justice and provide care for distant lands and peoples. Such consideration may require a great deal of imagination, particularly if members of the congregation have not traveled much beyond their local community. The fact that many churches believe that their resources have dwindled in the last fifty years may also stifle creative thinking. Invoking the old adage "charity begins at home" can become a way of ducking responsibility for God's people beyond our immediate view. In times of failed or failing vision, studying the apocalyptic book of Revelation may give mission, outreach, and social action boards new insights into God's desire to heal the world.

HYMN SING

Sing together "For the Healing of the Nations" (*CH,* 668; *UMH,* 428; *NCH,* 576). Note that this hymn is based on the concluding chapters of the biblical book of Revelation. Ask participants what they know about the Revelation to John. Explain that Revelation is an example of apocalyptic literature, writings that express a negative view of their contemporary culture and express a vision of an amazing new world in the future. It was written during a time when the early church was being threatened and its members persecuted for their beliefs. The words borrowed by the hymn are part of the early church's vision of how the world would be when God's realm replaced the corrupt and violent kingdom in which they lived and worshiped in fear for their lives.

BIBLE STUDY

Read *Revelation 21:1–4* with one person taking the part of the author and a second providing the "loud voice" that begins speaking midway through verse three. Share your reactions to the image of a "new heaven and a new earth" described in these verses. These questions may help you focus your conversation:

1. Who will reside in this new world?
2. What will be banished from this new world?
3. Would you want to be a part of this new society? Why or why not?

Now read *Revelation 22:1–5*. Work together to draw a picture of the image portrayed in this passage. Then discuss these questions:

1. What is the significance of the "river of the water of life"?
2. To whom do the river and the trees beside it belong?
3. Do you think access to the river and the trees are limited to those near God's throne? Why or why not?
4. How might the life-giving water of the river and the healing leaves of the tree be made available to those in need of life and healing?
5. How might our congregation help effect the healing of the nations and the coming of the new heaven and new earth?

Conclude your study by singing again the first stanza of "For the Healing of the Nations" as an intercessory prayer.

Options

Rather than singing the hymn, participants could simply read the words aloud or listen to a recording. The exercise of drawing the image presented in Revelation 22:1–5 may also be altered or even omitted. What these elements provide are other ways of interpreting the texts that depend less on literal thinking and more on imaginative thinking. Because the Revelation to John is a book filled with visions and coded symbolism, engaging it in imaginative ways helps participants enter into the literary style of the book and the imagination of the author.

Resource 6   *Finding a prophetic voice*

Every mission, outreach, or social action committee faces the challenging task of deciding which of the many assistance organizations and social causes will receive their congregation's attention. While denominational offering campaigns and pooled outreach funds may alleviate some local decision-making dilemmas, most churches engage in direct donations as well. So board members need to establish themselves as informed spokespersons capable of guiding the congregation as it decides how it will be a neighbor to those in need.

Committee members also need to articulate the variety of ways in which their congregation might act. Sometimes the needs of others are met best through actions that challenge systems or individuals who are oppressive. Other times congregations are called by God to support organizations that build up individuals and nurture compassion. Mission, outreach, and social action boards need to cultivate a close relationship with God that informs their knowledge of outreach opportunities and motivates them to speak plainly to their congregations about God's plans for the world. The story of Jeremiah's call to be a prophet can help them embrace their own prophetic voices.

BIBLE STUDY

Read *Jeremiah 1:4–10* aloud as a dialogue between Jeremiah and God. (Jeremiah reads verse 4, verse 6 and the first phrase of verse 7, and the first half of verse 9; God speaks the rest of the time.) Note that Jeremiah was a prophet of judgment, concerned with naming social ills that ought to be eradicated and condemning oppressive institutions that separated people from God's love. Think about how Jeremiah's calling and the work of your committee are related by exploring the following questions:

1. How well does God know Jeremiah?
2. Why is God certain that Jeremiah can be a successful prophet?
3. What are the two aspects of the message God gives to Jeremiah?
4. How do these two aspects (challenging unjust and immoral systems, creating just and godly systems) complement one another?
5. How might we encourage church members to both "pull down" and "build" in our congregation's outreach?
6. From where do we get our authority to commission such activities?

Take a few moments to identify some problematic activities or perspectives in your local community and/or the world community that need to be condemned and replaced with more just and compassionate actions and views. Pray that God will give you the words to express this need and motivate others to act.

Options

If committee members struggle with the idea that their work is a call to prophesy, acknowledge their struggle by reading Jeremiah's own laments in Jeremiah 11:18—12:17. In this passage are two of Jeremiah's heartfelt complaints about the nature and risk of his work and God's reassurance that messages of justice do eventually result in changes in the world. Note that our work for justice can be painful, both because our friends and neighbors sometimes refuse to support us and because our efforts can seem inadequate. Lament together the ways in which our world continues to fall short of being God's realm despite God's past work and present promises.

Resource 7 *God works through God's people to change the world*

Most mission, outreach, and social action boards are all too familiar with the excuses church members make to avoid participation in outreach projects. Some of these refusals stem from concerns about the nature and efficacy of outreach work. This resource is designed to help committees develop an appropriate response to these kind of excuses. It focuses on a familiar biblical figure—Mary, the mother of Jesus—and wrestles with the implications of her role in the coming of God's realm.

BIBLE STUDY

Read *Luke 1:26–38* as a dialogue between the angel Gabriel and Mary, with a narrator filling in the descriptions between their words. Think about the ways in which Mary is portrayed in the text. Ask yourselves,

1. How does God view Mary?
2. How does Mary initially characterize herself?
3. How does Mary describe herself after hearing Gabriel's response to her concern?

TRYING ON THE ROLE OF MARY

Ask the group to imagine that they are Mary. Invite them to sing Miriam Therese Winter's hymn "My Soul Gives Glory to My God" (*CH*, 130; *NCH*, 119; *UMH*, 198). Note that the hymn is based on Luke 1:46–55 and represents one part of Mary's response to Gabriel's message. Then discuss the following questions:

1. As Mary, how do you feel about your participation in God's work on earth?
2. What circumstances encourage you to rejoice in God's call to service?

Now imagine that some members of your congregation have just been confronted by Gabriel's announcement that they are called to serve God and help usher in God's realm. Develop a support strategy that will help them respond positively to this call by considering the following issues:

1. What concerns might the members of our congregation have about their ability to serve God?
2. How might we help them imagine that their call is a part of a larger initiative on God's part?
3. How might we remind them of God's past faithfulness and just actions?

Pray that God will help your committee keep these questions in mind when you are choosing and planning specific outreach opportunities.

Options

Instead of singing a hymn based on the song of Mary (known liturgically as the *Magnificat* for its first word in the Latin translation), read Luke 1:46–55 responsively. Several hymnals include such a reading set with a simple sung response that can be used or omitted (*CH,* 131; *NCH,* 732; *UMH,* 199). Or read this passage in unison from your favorite translation. Groups that particularly enjoy music might conclude their study by listening to a recording of John Michael Talbot's "St. Theresa's Prayer" (Birdwing Music, 1987). This piece emphasizes God's chosen dependence on human hands to do God's work on earth. Talbot also has a recording of the first half of Mary's song (Lk. 1:46–50) titled "Holy Is His Name" (Birdwing Music, 1980).

Resource 8   *Finding happiness in helping others*

Complaints about sixty-hour work weeks, a lack of family time, and unmet needs for personal relaxation make up the dominant set of excuses people give for avoiding outreach project commitments. Many church members view mission and social action events as activities that consume time and energy without giving much back in return, so they engage in such events only when they feel they have extra time and energy to spare from their ordinary pursuits. Even mission, outreach, and social action committee members can begin to feel overburdened when they lose sight of the personal benefits of reaching out to others. Avoid this "burned out" feeling and rediscover the joy of outreach with this celebration of Psalm 146.

PRAYER

Ask participants to think silently about the aspects of the committee's work that they find most burdensome. Tell them that you will be inviting them to share these burdens briefly in prayer after two minutes of silence. Pause for silent reflection, then pray using this form:

> Loving and compassionate God, we gather to do your work with some reluctance. The difficulty of making time and finding energy for our planning responsibilities

and our outreach activities weighs us down. Hear us now as we name aloud and silently the particular burdens we feel. (*Pause so that participants can name their burdens.*) We need you to refresh and renew us, God. Help us to rediscover the joy of our service in your name. Amen.

RESPONSIVE READING

Stand and divide into two groups. Ask each group to imagine that the other group has never experienced God's help and that their job in the next few minutes is to convince one another that God is an awesome God. Join in the following responsive reading of *Psalm 146,* using your voices to convey to one another the amazement and excitement this recital of God's wondrous deeds might generate.

> All: **Praise the Lord!**
> **Praise the Lord, O my soul!**
> Leader: I will praise the Lord as long as I live;
> I will sing praises to my God all my life long.
> Group 1: Do not put your trust in princes,
> in mortals, in whom there is no help.
> Group 2: When their breath departs, they return to the earth; on that very day their plans perish.
> Leader: Happy are those whose help is the God of Jacob,
> whose hope is in the Lord their God,
> Group 1: who made heaven and earth, the sea, and all that is in them;
> Group 2: who keeps faith forever;
> Group 1: who executes justice for the oppressed;
> Group 2: who gives food to the hungry.
> Group 1: The Lord sets the prisoners free;
> Group 2: the Lord opens the eyes of the blind.
> Group 1: The Lord lifts up those who are bowed down;
> Group 2: the Lord loves the righteous.

> Leader: The Lord watches over the strangers;
> Group 1: God upholds the orphan and the widow,
> Group 2: but the way of the wicked God brings to ruin.
> Leader: The Lord will reign forever,
> your God, O Zion, for all generations.
> All: **Praise the Lord!**

At the conclusion of the reading, ask participants to share how their experience of this psalm has affected their emotions and energy level. Do participants feel happy (v. 5) after enthusiastically declaring the ways in which God is working in the world? Do they feel motivated to work with God in the ways described in verses 7–9? If this exercise has been effective in lifting the sense of burdensomeness from the group's shoulders, ask if the group would like to try beginning future meetings in this manner. If the exercise did not alleviate the group's sense of overload, then brainstorm other approaches to finding happiness in working alongside our God.

Options

For some board members, the reason for feeling overburdened may in fact be that they are carrying too much responsibility for the work of the group or the congregation. In this case, focusing on the actions of God and the happiness that comes from being helped by God (in unseen ways and through the actions of others who take on new responsibilities) may be more useful than exploring the happiness that comes from working beside God. Both receiving God's aid and actively putting our trust to work with God are aspects of the God-human relationship in Psalm 146.

Resource 9 *Outreach and church growth*

Church growth is an important aspect of congregational survival. Every committee should think seriously about the ways in which their work promotes both the spiritual and numeric growth of the body of Christ. While outreach activities should not become thinly veiled attempts at congregational self-promotion, such activities should be expected to remind people of God's love and kindle in them a desire to celebrate that love with others. The Hebrew prophets believed that just actions done in God's name would eventually draw those who deemed God irrelevant in their lives back into the community of faith. We also live in a time when many fail to see the relevance of God and participation in church life. Use this resource to imagine how your mission, outreach, or social action committee might become a "repairer of the breach" between God and humanity.

INTRODUCTION

Ask participants why they think people today find participation in church life unattractive. List the reasons they give on a piece of newsprint posted on the wall.

BIBLE STUDY

Read *Isaiah 58:9b–12*. Explore the following questions:

1. What problems does the prophet identify? (Note: The "yoke" in verse 9 likely means the burden of unnecessary and/or rigid rules and rituals that prevent people from engaging in meaningful religious practices.)
2. What should be the work of the community of faith?
3. What happens when the community engages in the work God has set before it?
4. Why will meeting the pressing needs of others contribute to the rebuilding of the church? (Think about the impact on those within the congregation as well as on those outside the church walls.)
5. If our congregation follows the advice of Isaiah, in what ways might our work challenge the perceptions people have about church that keep them from joining?

Post a second piece of newsprint on the wall with the phrase "a light rising in the darkness" inscribed on it. As your committee moves through its agenda for this meeting, ask yourselves whether the decisions you are making contribute to your congregation's light or to the darkness that turns people away from the church.

Options

This resource can also be used to examine the efficacy of all the outreach activities a committee or board has planned for the year. Create or distribute a list of your group's outreach plans. Post two sheets of newsprint on the wall and label one sheet "increases our light" and the other "contributes to darkness." Work through the list item by item, discussing the ways in which each activity illustrates God's love and compassion for the afflicted and/or contributes to people's view of the church as a rigid, demanding, judgmental community. Don't be surprised if some activities send mixed messages. Use your findings to restructure or replace activities that offer little light and to reinforce your commitment to those activities that shine forth like the noonday sun.

Resource 10   *Ministry to prisoners*

While some congregations gravitate to prison ministries, many mission, outreach, and social action boards have trouble generating any sympathy or concern for those imprisoned. Our current cultural bias encourages a retribution approach to those convicted of crimes, nurtured in part by the sensational portrayals of violent crime and drug abuse in the news and entertainment industries. Congregations wonder why they should share their limited outreach resources with those who have brought their suffering upon themselves, when so many more worthy "victims" need help.

The apostle Paul offers an answer to this silent (or not so silent) query among people of faith. In his letter to the Romans, he demonstrates how a congregation's commitment to "bless those who persecute" them can help usher in God's realm. If your committee or board hasn't identified prison ministry as one of its concerns already, or if others are challenging your commitment to this kind of ministry, let Paul help you understand why this ministry is so important.

INTRODUCTION

Explain that the group is going to engage in a Bible study that explores a passage written for a specific historical situation (as most scripture was) and applies it to a related—but not identical—situation in our time. Ask participants to listen for the ways in which the passage can inform this new situation rather than looking for points of disparity between the two situations. Explain that such points of disparity may be accurate, but the writers of the Bible hoped that their readers would learn to apply the same theological perspective to new situations as well.

BIBLE STUDY

Read *Romans 12:14–21* aloud, with either one person reading the entire passage or each participant taking a verse. Suggest that persons who have been convicted of a crime are people accused of persecuting society with their unlawful actions. These persons are, in effect, our "enemies." Using this definition of "those who persecute you," discuss the following questions:

1. How are we expected to treat those convicted of crimes?
2. Why does Paul advise us to have compassion for our "enemies"?
3. Why must we "leave room for the wrath of God" instead of exacting our own vengeance?
4. How might we provide for the hunger and thirst of prisoners, both in literal and spiritual terms?

End your study by looking through the day's newspaper for articles about those accused of crimes and praying together for those individuals that their inclination to do wrong might be overcome by God's goodwill.

Options

To save time during the meeting, clip the newspaper articles beforehand. To expand this study, add a musical component by singing "Your Ways Are Not Our Own" (*NCH*, 170), a hymn based on the Romans passage. Further expand your exploration of the topic by seeking out someone in your congregation or community who has been imprisoned or has visited with someone in prison. Invite that person to share his or her experience with the group and to reflect with you about the meaning and practical application of Paul's advice. If someone is not readily available to meet with your group, read and discuss "Keeping Faith on Both Sides of the Fence" (*The Disciple*, Nov. 1997), which provides a brief reflection on my own struggle around this issue while corresponding with a younger brother incarcerated for seven years in a Texas prison.

Chapter 7

Asking God to Serve on the Evangelism, Witness, and Church Growth Committees

Evangelism, or spreading the good news of God's love, is the task of every church member and every church committee or board. When churches create an evangelism, witness, or church growth committee, they are not taking away the responsibility to evangelize from the rest of the body of Christ. Rather, evangelism, witness, and church growth boards work to focus the congregation's attention and energy on the task of evangelism by developing a vision and strategies for effective communication of the gospel. They also develop methods for recruiting and incorporating new church members from among those they evangelize. They are leaders in spreading the good news, and they are also the voice of Jesus saying to their congregations, "The harvest is plentiful, but the laborers are few; therefore ask the Lord of the harvest to send out laborers into his harvest" (Lk. 10:2).

Of course, recruiting laborers who are willing to get their hands dirty working in the neighborhood "field" is hard work in and of itself. Some church members, anxious to avoid appearing foolish, insensitive, or fanatical, shy away from evangelistic activities. They reason that the presence of their church building in the area—and the nice sign out front—should be sufficient to attract new members. Congregations in which the majority of members hold this viewpoint are likely to have "membership" or church growth boards that focus on recruiting members once prospects walk through the door. Other members readily invite their friends and neighbors to visit a service of worship or special church event but emphasize the social benefits of membership rather than the gospel challenge to become disciples of Christ. Still others believe that evangelism is vitally important, yet they hesitate to share the good news with others because they don't know how to do so effectively. Evangelism, witness, and church growth committees help church members make contemporary sense of Christ's command to "go therefore and make disciples of all nations, baptizing them in the name of the Father and of the Son and of the Holy Spirit, and teaching them to obey everything that I have commanded you" (Mt. 28:19–20). They seek to identify and respectfully dismantle all the barriers to fulfilling the great commission erected by their congregations.

Evangelism, witness, and church growth boards have much in common with mission, outreach, and social action committees. All these groups encourage church members to think about the world beyond the sanctuary as populated with people loved by God and in need of God's mercy. Therefore, the resources provided in chapter 6 are useful for evangelism, witness, or church growth boards. But what makes these committees different is their explicit emphasis on extolling the benefits of church participation for those seeking spiritual sustenance. This emphasis means that board members need to become public relations experts. They need to know the demographics of their neighborhoods and be able to name the ways in which their congregations can meet the spiritual needs of their communities. Committee members also may have to become internal change agents if they discover that their congregations' ministries have little to offer their neighbors. Such arduous and sometimes risky work demands that evangelism, witness, and church growth board members pay careful attention to their spiritual well-being so they will not tire of their labor of love.

+ + +

Resource 1   *The work of an evangelist*

We cannot be evangelists if we do not know what constitutes the work of an evangelist. How, then, do we figure this out? We could simply turn on the Christian Broadcasting Channel and claim television evangelists as our models or think back to the last time someone came knocking on our door with religious tracts in hand. After all, these are the people who claim to understand and practice the kind of evangelism needed in contemporary times, and they may indeed be faithful evangelists. Those who are faithful likely take their inspiration and guidance from the letters of the experienced evangelist Paul to Timothy, a young evangelist mentored by Paul in the early church. Evangelism, witness, and church growth committees can turn to this same source as they seek to equip members of their congregations as twenty-first-century evangelists.

BIBLE STUDY

Ask one person to read aloud *2 Timothy 4:1–5*. Generate on newsprint a list of attributes and actions that this passage associates with being an evangelist. Then discuss these questions:

1. Why does an evangelist need these attributes and engage in these actions? (Attend to verses 3–4 as well as your own experiences when answering this question.)
2. What are the "teachers" and "myths" that distract people in our local community from the truth?
3. How might our congregation proclaim the gospel in ways that are convincing? That rebuke? That encourage? That evidence patience?

Ask participants to sit quietly for two or three minutes and imagine these kinds of proclamations happening in your local community. After silently reflecting together, ask participants to share their images with the group. Affirm both positive images and those that contain elements of fear and anxiety. Conclude your sharing time by inviting participants to offer prayers of hope and concern for your congregation's ministry of evangelism.

Options

Carry the practical implications of this study further by working together to identify persons in your congregation who exemplify the characteristics of an evangelist and discussing ways your committee might encourage these persons to embrace such a calling and then sustain them in their work. Sing together the hymn "I Love To Tell the Story" (*CH*, 480; *UMH*, 156; *NCH*, 522) either after or in place of the closing prayer. If participants have concerns about the public image of evangelists (borne, perhaps, of negative past experiences with evangelism attempts), discuss these concerns during the Bible study, especially during consideration of question 3.

Resource 2 *The problem with "idols"*

Part of the task of evangelism is naming our human dependence on God. Despite the marketing claims of North American advertisers, people do not find happiness and fulfillment in the many "things" available for purchase. Nor is self-help therapy sufficient to address the human longing for security and meaning. We can create many "idols" that receive our loyalty and assuage our fears. The scriptures and Christian tradition both tell us, however, that placing our confidence in anything other than God leads to disappointment and the death of meaningful existence. Evangelism, witness, and church growth boards must repeatedly lift up the truth about idols and their failure to replace the life that God gives us. The vivid images of the prophet Habakkuk can help.

LITANY OF SCRIPTURE

Proclaim together the words of *Habakkuk 2:18–20* using the following litany:

Leader: What use is an idol once its maker has shaped it—a cast image, a teacher of lies?

People: **For its maker trusts in what has been made, though the product is only an idol that cannot speak!**

Leader: Alas for you who say to the wood,

People: **"Wake up!"**

Leader: to silent stone,

People: **"Rouse yourself!"**

Leader: Can it teach?
See, it is gold and silver plated,
and there is no breath in it at all.

All: **But the Lord is in God's holy temple; let all the earth keep silence before God!**

ENGAGING THE SCRIPTURES PRAYERFULLY

Ask participants to reread the passage silently to themselves, and then to meditate on the passage by imagining themselves creating an image that represents something dear to them and noticing the ways in which their image falls short of whatever it represents. After a few minutes of silent meditation, invite participants to share their imaginative experiences with the group.

When those who wish to share have done so, hand out pencils and index cards or pieces of paper to group members. Invite participants to read the text again silently, choosing a phrase that stands out to them as the words of a prayer they say silently over to themselves several times. Allow three or four minutes of silence for these prayers, then ask the members of the group to quiet their minds and wait in silence for God to respond in some way to their words of prayer. Tell them that they may wish to write or draw God's response on the card (paper) provided. After five minutes (or when activity ceases), invite the group to join you in a brief closing prayer such as this one:

> God, you have drawn near to us in this place, and we give thanks for your wisdom and guidance in our lives. Bless us and keep us all our days, that we might dwell in your house forever. Amen.

Options

The process described above for engaging the scriptures prayerfully is an ancient practice called in Latin *lectio divina,* or holy (divine) reading. If this process is new to your group, consider omitting the meditation piece, moving instead from the litany to the rereading and repetitive prayer. This shortens the amount of time spent in silence. The group can also end the contemplative experience after the meditation sharing and explore questions such as,

1. How can we identify the "idols" in our congregational life and replace them with trust in God?
2. How can we identify societal "idols" and encourage those around us to relinquish them?
3. How can we help those around us appreciate the benefits of gathering with us to glorify God in worship?

Resource 3   *Inviting strangers into God's realm*

Congregations committed to church growth often spend time investigating the demographics of the neighborhoods surrounding their church buildings because they know that new members are mostly likely to come from nearby homes. What some congregations find distressing is the discovery that the people who live near them do not share the same social and/or cultural characteristics as their current members. A church populated by older adults may discover that young families with children occupy most of the neighborhood. A traditionally white, middle-class, urban congregation may be situated in a predominantly black neighborhood plagued by high unemployment rates. A small, rural, family-oriented church may notice that the surrounding towns have lost most of their young families, leaving only aging adults and a few teenagers as new member prospects. Faced with this information, congregations wonder whether they want to reach out to people different from themselves.

Even congregations whose neighbors look and act like them may discover that the people they are recruiting for membership have little interest in church life. In all these situations, evangelism, witness, and church growth committees must struggle with the issues of who needs to hear the gospel message, how the good news can be shared, and what happens when the message is received. They may need to assist their congregations in developing new visions and means of evangelism informed by the stories Jesus told. This resource explores a story about a banquet that Jesus told to the Pharisees.

DRAMATIC READING OF SCRIPTURE

Invite several people to play the parts of the characters in the story of the banquet recorded in *Luke 14:12–24*. Each character reads her or his part with as much feeling and dramatic flair as she or he can muster.

Narrator: Jesus was dining with a leader of the Pharisees and several of that man's friends on the Sabbath. He said to the one who had invited him,

Jesus: When you give a luncheon or a dinner, do not invite your friends or your brothers or your relatives or rich neighbors, in case they may invite you in return, and you would be repaid. But when you give a banquet, invite the poor, the crippled, the lame, and the blind. And you will be blessed, because they cannot repay you,

<table>
<tr><td></td><td>for you will be repaid at the resurrection of the righteous.</td></tr>
<tr><td>Narrator:</td><td>One of the dinner guests, on hearing this, said to him,</td></tr>
<tr><td>Guest:</td><td>Blessed is anyone who will eat bread in the kingdom of God!</td></tr>
<tr><td>Narrator:</td><td>Then Jesus said to him,</td></tr>
<tr><td>Jesus:</td><td>Someone gave a great dinner and invited many. At the time for the dinner he sent his slave to say to those who had been invited,</td></tr>
<tr><td>Slave:</td><td>Come, for everything is ready now.</td></tr>
<tr><td>Jesus:</td><td>But they all alike began to make excuses. The first said to him,</td></tr>
<tr><td>Invitee 1:</td><td>I have bought a piece of land, and I must go out and see it; please accept my regrets.</td></tr>
<tr><td>Jesus:</td><td>Another said,</td></tr>
<tr><td>Invitee 2:</td><td>I have bought five yoke of oxen, and I am going to try them out; please accept my regrets.</td></tr>
<tr><td>Jesus:</td><td>Another said,</td></tr>
<tr><td>Invitee 3:</td><td>I have just been married, and therefore I cannot come.</td></tr>
<tr><td>Jesus:</td><td>So the slave returned and reported this to his master. Then the owner of the house became angry and said to his slave,</td></tr>
<tr><td>Master:</td><td>Go out at once into the streets and lanes of the town and bring in the poor, the crippled, the blind, and the lame.</td></tr>
<tr><td>Jesus:</td><td>And the slave said,</td></tr>
<tr><td>Slave:</td><td>Sir, what you ordered has been done, and there is still room.</td></tr>
<tr><td>Jesus:</td><td>Then the master said to the slave,</td></tr>
<tr><td>Master:</td><td>Go out into the roads and lanes, and compel people to come in, so that my house may be filled. For I tell you, none of those who were invited will taste my dinner.</td></tr>
</table>

BIBLE STUDY

Ask participants to find the Luke passage in their Bibles, or provide each one with a copy of the dramatic reading. Discuss the following questions:

1. Who does Jesus say we should invite to join our community of faith? (This can seem like a trick question because of the way the story begins in verse 12 and again because of the statement in verse 24. Help participants distinguish between who may be invited and the motivations of the one inviting or the responses of those asked to come. The next two questions help with these distinctions.)

2. What makes invitations to friends and relatives problematic?

3. What do the "excuses" offered by the first people invited say about their interest in participating? (If necessary, point out that each excuse is irrational. People in Jesus' time would not have bought land sight unseen or purchased oxen without trying them out in advance. Members of the same communities did not schedule big parties close to wedding celebrations, so the third man's marriage could not have been recent enough to preclude his coming.)

4. Why does Jesus counsel the religious leaders of his time to focus their recruitment efforts on the poor and needy?

5. Who are the poor and needy in our neighborhood? (Encourage participants to include spiritual poverty and neediness in their responses.)

6. How might our congregation offer a compelling invitation to participate in the body of Christ to the people we have identified?

Conclude with prayer for God's strength and guidance as your congregation goes into the streets and lanes of your local community with the message of God's grace and provision.

Options

If your board or committee is particularly concerned about church growth for the sake of financial survival, focus participants' attention on the "excuses" offered by the financially secure when asked to fulfill their commitments to the banquet host. Explain that banquets in Jesus' time involved long and costly preparations, so hosts generally issued invitations specifying a general time frame for the gathering well in advance and then prepared for those who had responded affirmatively. When the preparations for the banquet were completed, the host then sent for all who had agreed to come. To refuse the second invitation was to indicate that one had little value or regard for the host. Discuss how this story situation might inform your own expectations about the commitment of persons recruited primarily for their financial contributions. Ask yourselves,

1. How might we address the spiritual needs of prospective and new members so that they will want to support the life of this congregation?
2. What might be the dangers of a recruitment process that emphasizes a congregation's financial "poverty" rather than its spiritual "wealth"?

Resource 4 *Shining God's light in the world*

Evangelism, witness, and church growth boards may, at times, feel overwhelmed by the magnitude of their task. Organizing people to "go into all the world and make disciples" in Christ's name is hard work, especially if the importance of their task is disputed, the prospective laborers are often "too busy" to follow through, and the recipients of the good news seem uninterested in—even hostile to—the message. When discouragement threatens to overcome the sense of purpose necessary to effective leadership, let the prophet Isaiah restore hope among committee members as he did among the people of Israel.

SCRIPTURE READING

Ask someone with a strong voice to read *Isaiah 60:1–3* as if she or he were trying to awaken someone from a deep sleep. Ask someone else to read the same passage in a loud whisper as if he or she were sharing a powerful secret. (Solicit these volunteers before your meeting, so that others do not hear your instructions to them.) Then ask everyone to stand and read the passage aloud in unison as if they claiming the words for themselves. (Provide participants with the same translation of the Bible or copies of the scripture reading.)

DISCUSSION

Invite people to share their responses to the various readings.

1. How did the various readings make you feel?
2. What words in the passage caught your attention? Why?
3. What is your reaction to the news that our light comes from God's glory, not from ourselves?
4. How do we imagine ourselves "shining" in ways that reflect God's glory?
5. How might the promise of verse 3 encourage us in our work?

HYMN SINGING

Invite participants to sing either "We've a Story to Tell to the Nations" (*CH*, 484; *UMH*, 569) or "I Am the Light of the World" (*CH*, 469; *NCH*, 584) as a testimony to God's glory and an act of recommitment to the work of evangelism.

Options

Churches experiencing a crisis of vision and identity might use this resource as part of a congregational meeting or service of worship to refocus and reenergize their members. The first reader might begin shouting from the back of the room (sanctuary) and move to the front while he or she speaks; the second reader might move through the assembly, whispering the words to groups of people and motioning for them to stand in preparation for the unison reading. Participants can be invited to read in unison from pew Bibles, from printed handouts, or from words projected before them.

In any setting, a candle or lantern might be carried in or lit as the first reader speaks. The second reader might then offer participants candles lit from the original candle (the Christ light) or small mirrors to hold so that they reflect the light of the lantern. Participants would continue to hold their candles or mirrors while they rise and read in unison, then would place these items on a central table with the original candle or lantern as symbols of God's light multiplying through our participation in God's work.

Resource 5   *Nurturing the seeds we sow*

Evangelism will not lead to church growth if evangelism, witness, and church growth boards do not take with equal seriousness the tasks of sharing the gospel and of nurturing the faith formation of those who receive this good news. While no one can force an individual to allow the gospel to transform every aspect of her or his life, these committees can foster a congregational climate that encourages newcomers to plant themselves in soil fertile with possibilities for faith formation. A fresh look at Jesus' parable of the sower can help evangelism, witness, and church growth committee members envision ways to accomplish this task.

BIBLE STUDY

Ask one person to read *Matthew 13:1–9* and a second to read *Matthew 13:18–23*. As a group, make a list on newsprint of those things that prevent God's word from flourishing in the lives of those who hear it. For example, the birds or "the evil one" might be characterized on the list as "other value messages that compete for people's allegiance." The rocky ground might be interpreted as "failure to obtain a deep grounding in scripture" and/or "failure to be firmly connected to the faith community."

The thorns might represent a "lack of a spiritual discipline to guide one's life" or an "inability to apply scriptural teaching to everyday life."

Once the group has created a list of several "problems" that can plague new church members (and perhaps many longtime members as well), discuss the following questions:

1. How might we turn each of these problems into opportunities for growth?
2. Which other committees (boards) need to assist us in creating these opportunities?
3. How might we encourage newcomers to take advantage of these opportunities?

Close with a prayer asking God to help you prepare good soil that will enable those who are drawn to your congregation through its evangelistic efforts to have fruitful Christian lives.

Options

Invite participants to sing "Almighty God, Your Word Is Cast" (*NCH*, 318), which is based on the parable of the sower, as their closing prayer. The hymn "How Firm a Foundation" (*CH*, 618; *UMH*, 529; *NCH*, 407), which emphasizes the importance of scripture in grounding the lives of Christians, is also appropriate. For congregations and committees intrigued by the relationship between understanding the word and bearing fruit (the description given in verse 23 of the effects of "good soil"), the hymn "Sent Forth by God's Blessing" (*UMH*, 664; *NCH*, 76) offers ideas about how this connection looks in practice. Participants might both sing the hymn text and discuss how they might help newcomers engage in the particular actions it encourages.

Chapter 8

Asking God to Serve on the Congregational Life and Parish Care Committees

An important way that a congregation moves from being a simple collection of individuals to a community of faith with vision and purpose is by attending to the quality of their common life together. As we eat together, cry together, celebrate together, and talk about ordinary events together, we develop networks of relationships that contribute to our sense of security and "at-home-ness" in the church. A rich and faithful congregational life lends authenticity to the claim we make in the hymn "Blest Be the Tie That Binds," in which we sing, "the fellowship of kindred minds is like to that above." Our participation in the body of Christ becomes an experience of heavenly communion with God and a foretaste of God's realm on earth.

This foretaste of glory divine, however, is not solely for the purpose of feeling "at home" in a religious setting that meets our personal needs for positive social relationships and emotional security. Christians create a life together in order to nurture and sustain themselves in the service to which they have been called by God. The sanctuary of fellowship creates the necessary safe space within which we can challenge ourselves (and be challenged by others) to identify and act on God's expectations for us. The comfort of caring relationships enables us to risk being all that God has created us to be.

106

The primary task, then, of congregational life and parish care committees is to nurture the common life of their congregations in ways that promote a community of disciples motivated to praise God and serve one another and the world. They assess the relational needs of their congregations and identify what kinds of nurturing are required at any particular time. One such committee may conclude that its congregation's well-being requires the development of a "coffee hour" after worship, provisions for child care during committee meetings, quarterly healing services, a system for delivering meals in times of need, prayer chains, and opportunities for conflict resolution training. Another may decide that quarterly neighborhood gatherings, monthly "parents' night out" events, a fellowship time between worship services, and the establishment of a lay pastoral care team will best support a rich community life for its church's members. There can be as many ways of nurturing faithful and fruitful community relationships as there are members of congregational life and parish care boards who enjoy creating them.

+ + +

Resource 1 *Communal hospitality*

We live in a highly mobile society, which means, among other things, that former members of other churches are moving into our neighborhoods all the time. These are people who are predisposed to church membership, having already been members somewhere else, and they often go "church shopping" once the moving boxes are unpacked. We might hope that their primary concern when visiting churches is the quality of the preaching or the depth of educational opportunities, and these issues do interest many visitors. But often what a visitor most remembers from a church visit is the kind of welcome she or he received from the congregation. This resource helps congregational life and parish care committees discover a key tool for welcoming newcomers in God's name.

BIBLE STUDY

Ask someone who's not intimidated by difficult-to-pronounce biblical names to read *Romans 16:1–15*. Then ask the group,

1. What is Paul asking the members of the Roman church to do?

Note that early Christians often traveled around to transact business or to avoid persecution in a region. Ask participants to help you make a list on newsprint of all the people Paul wants the church to greet, adding a one- or two-word description of each person next to her or his name. Then continue your discussion using the following questions:

2. How can we quickly get to know visitors so that we can greet them in the personal way that Paul describes? (Think about ways to learn visitors' names and something of their life experiences.)
3. How might we welcome visitors in ways that show we view them as people who have gifts to share with us? (Note that sharing a sense of congregational desperation for new members is likely to appeal only to those visitors who enjoy the "rescuer" role.)
4. What might a job description for congregational "greeters" look like?

Pray for recent and future visitors to your congregation, giving thanks for their presence among you and asking God's help in making them feel welcome in your church.

Options

Expand your work with this resource by developing a training program for congregational "greeters" based on the job description you created in response to question 4. End your discussion time with a hymn that proclaims the theme of welcome. Good hymns for this purpose include "Gather Us In" (*CH*, 284), "We Are the Church" (*UMH*, 558), and "We Are

Your People" (*NCH*, 309). Discuss what kind(s) of visual symbols your congregation might use to welcome newcomers. Ask an artistic church member to design this visual symbol of welcome, and place it near the church entrance most commonly used by visitors.

Resource 2 *Shared servanthood*

The gospel of John tells the story of the Last Supper with different details than the other gospels. Only in the Fourth Gospel do we hear about Jesus' going from one disciple to another and washing their feet. The church has taken its image of "servant leadership" from this image, and it is an image that congregational life and parish care boards can use to encourage a sense of shared servanthood among the members of their congregations. When committee members review this story together, they can reclaim its power for their particular community of disciples.

PRAYER

Invite participants to share briefly about the events of their day. Then pray for the group, giving thanks for the positive reports and asking God's comfort and help for those who are experiencing difficulties.

BIBLE STUDY

Read *John 13:1–17* in parts. Ask someone to take the part of Jesus, a second person to be Peter, and a third to narrate. Explain that foot washing was a common practice in the first century. Everyone's feet would be dirty from walking dusty roads in sandals, so the practice was to wash them before sitting down to dinner. During Passover, when Jews celebrated their deliverance from slavery in Egypt, they would take special care to wash and wear their finest clothes as a sign of their worth in God's eyes. If a family had slaves or servants, it was a slave's job to draw the water and kneel before each family member to wash his or her feet. Thus, Jesus is taking on the role of a slave or servant in this story.

Note that this story is packed with meaning. Suggest that the group focus their attention on the aspects of the story that help them answer the following questions:

1. Why does Jesus take on the role of a servant or slave? (If necessary, note that verses 8 and 12–16 will be most helpful in answering this and the other questions that focus on the story itself.)
2. What does Jesus tell the disciples they should do?
3. Why does Jesus want them to act in this way?
4. How can contemporary Christians "wash one another's feet"?
5. How can our committee (board) help facilitate these activities?

End your discussion by singing "Jesu, Jesu" (*CH,* 600; *UMH,* 432; *NCH,* 498) as a closing prayer.

Options

Most hymnals have a topical index with a section titled "Service" or "Discipleship." Use this list to identify other hymns that participants might sing to reinforce the theme of servant-hood. Design a litany for the installation of congregational leaders based on your reflections on this story, and share this litany with the persons responsible for such events. Give participants cutouts of feet and ask them to write a congregational need on each foot. Then brainstorm ways that you can encourage church members to care for these feet (needs) as Jesus did.

Resource 3 *Celebrating major events*

Christmas, Easter, and (in some churches) Pentecost are the major events of the church year, at least according to the liturgical calendar. Other events, like the kick-off of the fall programming schedule or the congregation's anniversary, carry substantial symbolic weight in the life of God's people as well. Religious people like to mark the most significant times in their lives with religious rituals. This practice of elevating certain days or passages is mentioned even in the earliest stories of the community of faith.

What these early stories also tell us is that religious celebrations can be sources of conflict as well as joy. Sometimes God's people disagree about the ways an event ought to be commemorated or the activities that Christians can include in their celebrations. Nothing kills the joyous momentum of a celebration planning process more quickly than a fight over the details of the event! And nothing undermines the pleasant memories of a wonderful celebration more easily than a few critical comments suggesting that something about the event wasn't right.

This resource encourages congregational life and parish care committees to think about the realities of event planning in ways that help them to focus more on the importance of congregational celebrations and less on the inevitable dissenting voices. Its purpose is not to suggest that disagreements over activities should be ignored, but to provide a forum in which committee members can set priorities for events and deal with criticism in relation to those priorities.

SINGING

Begin by singing some of your congregation's favorite praise songs or choruses. Songs like "Halle-Halle-Halleluja" (*CH,* 41; *NCH,* 236); "Masithi" (*CH,* 30; *NCH,* 760), "Blessed Be the Name" (*UMH,* 63), and "Clap Your Hands" (*CH,* 38) are good choices. When the joy of praising God has lifted the energy of the group into an enthusiastic working mode, invite participants to explore a biblical story of praise and celebration by their forebears in the faith.

BIBLE STUDY

Ask one person to read *2 Samuel 6:1–5,* a second to read *2 Samuel 6:16–19,* and a third to read *2 Samuel 6:20–22.* Ask participants if they remember the significance of the ark—why the Israelites had it and what it contained. If necessary, remind them that the ark represents the Israelites' covenant with God and contains the tablets of the Ten Commandments, some manna from the days of Israel's wandering in the wilderness, and Aaron's priestly staff. (If you would like more information about the ark, consult a Bible dictionary.) Focus your discussion on these questions:

1. Why are David and the people so excited? (One reason is that the bringing of the ark into Jerusalem marks the creation of a new nation devoted to the worship of God.)
2. How do the people show their enthusiasm? (Don't forget to look at verses 17–19 as well as the earlier verses.)
3. Why does Michal dislike David's behavior? Why is she a spectator rather than a participant?
4. How did David respond to Michal's concerns?
5. Can we imagine some ways that David and the others might have encouraged Michal to join in the celebration?
6. What are the principles that guide our decisions about the activities we engage in when we celebrate?
7. How can we avoid giving up these principles when someone thinks that other criteria (past experience, stricter behavioral norms) should govern our planning?

Options

Non-singers can begin by naming circumstances or events in their lives for which they praise God or by listening to a recording of praise music while sharing a simple festive snack. The goal is to study the story of the ark's movement to Jerusalem from a personal place of excitement and praise, rather than entering the story caught up in the cares of the world, which may have been part of Michal's problem.

Consider making a list of the principles that guide your board's planning process and publishing this list in your church newsletter. Explain to other members the reasons for these principles, and invite people to share their responses. Encourage members to evaluate congregational celebrations in light of their adherence to these principles.

Resource 4 *Celebrating our salvation together*

Many congregations excel at potluck dinners and pitch-in luncheons. Singles groups, women's circles, and men's breakfast clubs abound. Youth groups know well the value of pizza, bowling, and amusement park trips for their social life. Coffee hour may be more popular than the service of worship on Sunday mornings! It is great to socialize with our friends in the church, and these times of fellowship help bind us together as the people of God.

It is good to celebrate our friendships, and yet there is much more we need to celebrate as a community of faith. The church year offers us several special days for commemoration and celebration. In fact, the Bible tells us about several occasions when God commanded God's people to have a party! That God loves a celebration may be one of the best-kept secrets in Christianity. Congregational life and parish care committees can help get the word out once they discover this truth for themselves.

INTRODUCTION

Ask participants to name the top ten things that they believe God wants God's people to do. Put your list of ten on newsprint and post it on the wall.

BIBLE STUDY

Ask participants to find the book of Zechariah in the Bible. (Zechariah is the next to the last book in the Hebrew Scriptures, right before Malachi.) Explain that Zechariah was a prophet during the rebuilding of the temple in the sixth century B.C.E. Invite a participant to read *Zechariah 8:14–19*. Discuss the following question:

1. What are the five things that Zechariah tells the people to do? (Four are contained in verses 16–17; the fifth is found in verse 19.)

Explain that the months referred to in verse 19 are the months in which Jerusalem was attacked and eventually destroyed by the Babylonians. Discuss these questions:

2. Why does Zechariah tell the people to celebrate in these months? (One reason is that the events of the past have been reversed by God: What had "fallen" has been "lifted up.")
3. What kinds of activities might the people of Israel have used to celebrate God's deliverance and restoration of their community?
4. What divine acts of deliverance and restoration might Christians celebrate together? (Think about big holidays and more ordinary events in the history of the church as well as the particular events of your congregation's history and present life.)
5. How might we help our congregation recognize and celebrate (commemorate) these events?

Pick an event to commemorate and pray that God will help you plan a "festival" your congregation will never forget.

Options

The book of Psalms contains several celebratory songs praising God and recalling God's deliverance. Choose one of these psalms (e.g., Psalm 33; 100; 111; 113; 147–150) and read it responsively after discussing the Bible study questions. Psalm 100 is the inspiration for the hymn "All People That on Earth Do Dwell" (*CH,* 18; *UMH,* 75; *NCH,* 7); sing this hymn rather than reading a psalm. Or sing the Doxology ("Praise God from Whom All Blessings Flow") as a prelude to a closing prayer of thanks for all that God has done for us.

If the group is interested in hearing more about Zechariah's vision of how God's people will be reunited in celebration, read all of Zechariah 7—8 (37 verses). Chapter 7 explains that the people had been engaging in rituals of mourning and deprivation during the fifth month of the year, so Zechariah's statement that God wants them to celebrate instead is a huge surprise.

Resource 5 *Stewards of grace*

Church members tend to associate the term *stewardship* with pledge drives and raising money. The biblical concept of stewardship, however, is much broader and more complicated than our emphasis on money issues allows. The scriptures call on Christians to be stewards of many things, among them creation, money, the next generation, and their relationships with other Christians. Congregational life and parish care committees can explore the implications of this broader understanding of stewardship for their ministries by studying the first letter of Peter.

PRAYER

Begin by praying that God will help your group expand its understanding of stewardship. To do this, ask participants to state briefly their definitions of "stewardship" as you go quickly around the circle. Then pray these or similar words:

> God, we offer these definitions to you for expansion, revision, and further explanation. Open our ears to the scriptures and to one another, that we might learn all that it means to be stewards of your gifts. Amen.

BIBLE STUDY

Read aloud *1 Peter 4:7–11*. Note that these words were written to the Gentile (non-Jewish) Christians who lived in Asia Minor in the first century C.E. Many of these Christians were slaves or women married to nonbelieving husbands. They often suffered insults or abuse because of their commitment to Christ. This pastoral letter was intended to comfort and guide them as they struggled to keep their church together.

Use the following questions to guide discussion:

1. What are we called to be good stewards of?
2. How do we act as good stewards of God's grace?
3. Why is good stewardship so important?

Brainstorm ways that your board can encourage church members to serve one another with the gifts each has been given. Imagine ways that your committee can help church members tap into the "strength that God supplies."

Options

Some congregations have so many committees and activities that church members experience heavy demands on their time and energy that may not match their gifts and abilities. If this is the case in your congregation, ask yourselves these two additional questions:

1. How does our congregation sap "the strength that God supplies" out of our members?
2. What alternative ways of operating might we propose that would encourage better stewardship of the actual gifts people have, rather than pushing people into positions for which they feel ill-suited or prepared?

This resource, and the one that follows, also might be used by a congregation's stewardship or finance committee as part of an educational series on stewardship and its broad implications for congregational life.

Resource 6 *The relationship between giving and receiving*

Church members who grew up hearing that "it is more blessed to give than to receive" may have trouble sharing their needs and allowing others to serve them. They may feel that it is better to suffer in silence or muddle through independently, even though they are the first to step forward when someone else is in crisis. Congregational life and parish care boards can help such church members recognize that receiving another's help is a ministry of empowerment. Committee members can turn to Paul's letter to the church at Philippi for assistance in nurturing this understanding in their congregations.

BIBLE STUDY

Tell participants that one of the first churches established by the apostle Paul was the church at Philippi. Paul had a very close relationship with the members of that church. Note that the passage you will be studying comes from the end of Paul's letter to this church and explains a significant aspect of this relationship.

Ask one person to read *Philippians 4:10–14* and a second to read *Philippians 4:15–20*. Discuss the following questions:

1. How does Paul view his own needs and their fulfillment?
2. What is Paul's relationship with the church at Philippi?
3. What is "richness" or "wealth" for Paul?
4. What is the relationship between giving and receiving? (See especially verse 17.)
5. How is God connected to our giving and receiving?

Brainstorm ideas for communicating how a willingness to receive other people's gifts is a ministry that empowers others to be good stewards of the gifts God has given them. Pray that God will help your congregation hear this message and act on it.

Options

Consider beginning your meeting by asking how many people have heard the saying "It is better to give than to receive." Ask them what they think this saying means and where they think it comes from. After several people have shared their ideas, note that this saying is a common interpretation of the Bible's teaching, but it cannot be found as a specific verse in the

Bible. Suggest that what the Bible says about giving and receiving is actually more complicated than these simple words can capture. Then invite participants to examine Philippians 4:10–20 with you.

After the Bible study, encourage participants to come up with different sayings that express their new understanding of the relationship between giving and receiving. Consider making a poster or banner proclaiming this new saying and hanging your creation where church members will see it.

Resource 7 *Importance of community support in difficult times*

Although some people tend to keep their problems to themselves, having a friend in times of need is almost always preferable to facing a crisis alone. Even the most reticent person generally tells one or two close friends or family members about the struggles facing her or him. Both research and experience tell us that this kind of sharing is important to our mental, emotional, spiritual, and physical health. What experience also tells us is that most people are unlikely to share many details of their lives in a formal setting such as service of worship or in a large-group gathering such as coffee hour. The "prime time" events of church life do not promote the intimate sharing necessary for support networks to form.

We might be tempted to believe that sufficient sharing of personal concerns will occur without any help from us. We may assume that because church members are free to choose friends from among the people with whom they worship, surely they find one or two confidants to aid them in difficult times. This may indeed be true for some members of our congregations, but to leave such connections to chance overlooks an opportunity for ministry that could change some people's lives. Congregational life and parish care committees that want to explore more intentional forms of caregiving ministries can find a powerful rationale for their work in the book of Ecclesiastes.

INTRODUCTION

Ask participants to share some of the reasons they offer help to friends in need. Ask them to share some of the reasons they do or do not ask others for help in their own times of need. Invite them to explore a very brief biblical passage related to this topic of friends and needs.

BIBLE STUDY

Read *Ecclesiastes 4:9–12*. If the group is unfamiliar with the book of Ecclesiastes, tell them that this is the same book that contains the litany of time: "For everything there is a season, and a time for every matter under heaven: a time to be born, and a time to die..." (Eccl. 3:1–2a). It contains many reflections on the ordinary things of life and their meanings.

Divide the group into three smaller groups and ask each group to draw or dramatize the actions between friends described in this passage. Group 1 should focus on verse 10, group 2 on verse 11, and group 3 on verse 12. Give the groups five minutes to create their illustrations, then reassemble as one group and ask participants to share what they have created.

Discuss these illustrations and the passage as a whole with the help of the following questions:

1. What would happen if no one were around to help the fallen person? the cold person? the person who is threatened?
2. Why is working together (v. 9) more rewarding than working alone?
3. If we think of these passages as both literal and symbolic, what kinds of needs might be represented by these verses?
4. How might we encourage people in our congregation to share these needs with others who might lift them, surround them with warmth, and support them?

5. How might we train the members of our church to provide such ministries of caregiving?

Conclude your study with a time of prayer for all those
(known by name and unknown) in your congregation who have
particular need of congregational care.

Options

A group that prefers discussion to drama or drawing may
omit that activity and begin their conversation with the question, What are the three actions taken in verses 10 to 12? The
introductory exercise also may be omitted if time is short, or, if
time permits, it may be expanded to include a discussion of the
concepts of "independence," "dependence," "codependence,"
and "interdependence" and their relationship to our understandings of appropriate community support for those in need.

Resource 8 *Nurturing hope in the midst of despair*

Church members' personal struggles with job and family, as
well as their communally heightened awareness of violence and
suffering in the world, can lead to an increased sense of help-
lessness and despair. Congregations that struggle to keep their
doors open in the face of financial problems or community dis-
sent also risk seasons of despair among members worn out by
such hard work. And the increasing rate of suicide among youth
suggests that despair is a significant aspect of some young people's
lives. Congregational life and parish care boards may wonder
what their congregations can do to acknowledge despair and
prevent it from overwhelming those within the community of
faith. Let the words of hope proclaimed by the prophet Jeremiah
set a context for a committee discussion on this topic.

DRAMATIC BIBLE READING

Read *Jeremiah 31:7–9* using the following dramatic form:

Narrator: For thus says the Lord:

Male voice: Sing aloud with gladness for Jacob,

Female voice: and raise shouts for the chief of the nations; proclaim, give praise, and say,

All: **"Save, O Lord, your people, the remnant of Israel."**

Male voice: See, I am going to bring them from the land of the north,

Female voice: and gather them from the farthest parts of the earth,

Male voice: among them the blind and the lame,

Female voice: those with child and those in labor, together; a great company, they shall return here.

Male voice: With weeping they shall come, and with consolations I will lead them back,

Female voice: I will let them walk by brooks of water, in a straight path in which they shall not stumble;

Male voice: for I have become a father to Israel,

Female voice: and Ephraim is my firstborn.

DISCUSSION

Note that Jeremiah's words were addressed to the people while they remained in captivity during the Babylonian exile. The Israelites' future as a people looked grim; their removal from their homeland threatened to destroy their sense of community and undermined their reliance on God. Ask the following questions:

1. What does God say the people must do to change the situation? (See v. 7.)
2. What does God plan to do to make the situation better?
3. Who are the despairing in our congregation?
4. How can we gather with them and lift up their need for salvation from despair?

5. What do we want God to do to make the situation better?
6. How can we share our desires with these persons and with God in ways that nurture hopefulness?

Share with one another past experiences of despair that turned to hope as testimonies of God's faithfulness. Pray for those who despair, and commit yourselves to providing ministries of hopeful prayer and action for them.

Options

In conjunction with the discussion of Jeremiah, read the story of blind Bartimaeus in Mark 10:46–52. This gospel reading is paired with the Jeremiah passage in the prescribed readings of the Revised Common Lectionary. It models an assertive form of intercessory prayer in which persons in need speak plainly with God (and God's people) about what they lack and want.

Conclude by singing one of the many hymns that proclaim God's comfort and care for the afflicted. Perhaps the best-known hymn of this sort is "Amazing Grace" (*CH,* 546; *UMH,* 378; *NCH,* 547). Other well-known possibilities include "Precious Lord, Take My Hand" (*CH,* 628; *UMH,* 474; *NCH,* 472); "Sweet Hour of Prayer" (*CH,* 570; *UMH,* 496; *NCH,* 505), "There Is a Balm in Gilead" (*CH,* 501; *UMH,* 375; *NCH,* 553) "Be Still, My Soul" (*CH,* 566; *UMH,* 534; *NCH,* 488), and "His Eye Is on the Sparrow" (*CH,* 82; *NCH,* 475).

Resource 9 *Prayer and healing*

Healing services may seem to be primarily the concern of a congregation's worship committee and pastor or, in certain cases, an offshoot of an outreach ministry to persons living with AIDS or other life-threatening afflictions. The New Testament church, however, viewed the provision of healing as a critical part of congregational care. The church whose members were suffering was ill-prepared to go into all the world proclaiming the gospel. So the early church developed ministries of healing and expected their members to seek out these ministries when needed. Congregational life and parish care committees who want to expand their healing ministry focus can find one example of such a ministry in the book of James.

BIBLE STUDY

Ask two people to read *James 5:13–16*. The first person should read the questions in the text, while the second person reads the answers to the questions and the rest of the passage (vv. 15–16). Then discuss the following questions:

1. Why do you think church members are instructed to act in the ways described by verses 13–14?
2. What actions are included in the healing ritual? (If participants are unfamiliar with the practice of anointing sick persons with oil, consult a Bible commentary to help you explain the origins of this practice.)
3. What promise is made about prayer?
4. In what ways could prayer be powerful and effective even if the person prayed for is not cured? What other kinds of healing might occur?
5. How might our committee (board) encourage church members to seek healing?

Sing "O Christ, the Healer" (*CH,* 503; *UMH,* 265; *NCH,* 175) or "There Is a Balm in Gilead" (*CH,* 501; *UMH,* 375; *NCH,* 553) as a closing prayer and testimony of faith.

Options

Rather than singing a closing prayer, join hands and pray by name for the sick and afflicted in your congregation. If your board has decided that a healing service is one way it can encourage church members to seek healing, write a "Call to Healing" announcement or newsletter article sharing what you have learned from studying James. Make a poster that expresses your understanding of the difference between "healing" and "cure" and hang it in a prominent place in your church building. Invite someone who is living with chronic illness to talk with your committee about the person's understanding of healing and the resources he or she needs from the congregation to live as one healed but not cured.

Resource 10   *Offering hope to those who are dying and those who are grieving*

An essential ministry of the church is a ministry of comfort for the dying and the bereaved. Without such a ministry, the church misses an important opportunity to apply the good news of the resurrection in the most practical of ways: as a message of God's ability to overcome the power of death when death seems most powerful. Most congregations recognize the vital nature of this ministry, but many leave it solely in the hands of the clergy. An imaginative congregation, however, can devise many ways in which its members support and assist their pastor(s) in interpreting death and ministering to those touched by it. Congregational life and parish care committees can use this exploration of the concept of "dying well" to decide how they will help their congregations shape a ministry in partnership with their pastors.

INTRODUCTION

Read aloud *Psalm 23:4*. Invite participants to share their images of an ideal way to die. Emphasize that death is not an individual achievement to be judged, and encourage participants to respect each other's ideas. Note similarities and differences among the various preferences shared.

BIBLE STUDY

Ask participants to read *Romans 8:35–39* in unison. (Provide Bibles or copies of the text.) Point out that death, in its power to separate and alienate, is depicted as part of an old order. Discuss the following questions:

1. What is the new order?
2. What is our experience of death and separation?
3. How does our experience fit with the new order?

Note that we all die someday. Even though the "rescue" mentality of modern medicine works against our acceptance of dying, it is a fact of life that life ends. Invite participants to reread the Romans passage to themselves and to reflect silently for a minute on its meaning. Then ask,

4. What other kinds of hope can we offer dying persons besides the hope of elusive physical cures? These are some ideas that the group might want to consider:
    a. We can offer the living presence of God through our presence.
    b. We can proclaim the resurrection belief that love is stronger than death.
    c. We can offer the church as a community of memory (both of Jesus and of loved ones, the "communion of saints").
    d. We can embrace and care for family and friends as instruments of divine mercy.
    e. We can negotiate the tension between lament (grief) and hope (memories that live on).
    f. We can proclaim that death marks the point at which all temporal obstacles to the experience of God's love end.

Conclude your discussion by reciting or reading Psalm 23 together.

Options

Consider putting the list of ideas under question 4 on newsprint ahead of time and posting it for the group to discuss.

Modify any of the ideas as suggested by your conversation and add to the list ideas generated by the group. Expand the use of Psalm 23 by reading the passage and exploring the questions listed below before using the psalm as a unison prayer to conclude your study.

1. What is it about this passage that offers us comfort?
2. What do the images of "rod" and "staff" convey?

Other scripture passages on this topic that the group might explore are John 11:17–27 and Romans 14:7–9.

Chapter 9

Asking God to Serve on the Stewardship, Finance, and Property Committees

Talking about money makes some church members feel very uncomfortable, whereas others relish the power they wield as keepers of the church purse. Some church members conscientiously pay their stewardship pledges weekly, while others withhold their contributions when they are unhappy about a congregational decision or ministerial "attitude." Many people cringe if they hear the word "tithe" coming from the pulpit; some complain that tithing isn't given enough attention. Decisions about building improvements, staffing, programming, and outreach ministries all hinge on people's presuppositions about money and the spending of money. Therefore, those who serve on stewardship, finance, or property committees face the huge task of mediating congregational conversations about a topic few people want to discuss.

This task is further complicated by the biblical misinformation that people bring to the conversation. Many church members assume that the Bible demands that they "give until it hurts" and that the scriptures portray money as "evil." Yet out of more than two hundred references to money in the Bible, less than a third talk about giving money to religious bodies such as the church, and even fewer identify money as a negative influence. Most of the references talk about using money to meet personal or familial needs or pooling the community's money to take care of the social infrastructure. Stewardship, finance, and property boards must educate their congregations about the Bible's positive portrayal of money and help church members learn how to use their money wisely for the mutual benefit of themselves, their communities, and the church.

In addition to their shared goals of mediating conversations about church finances and providing biblical information about the role of money in our lives, stewardship, finance, and property committees have specific goals related to their particular monetary concerns. Stewardship committees seek to interpret the church's budget to people so that church members will make a commitment to the programmatic vision of the congregation. Finance committees work to develop and articulate financial policies and budget proposals that reflect their congregations' theological beliefs and support their churches' ministries. Property committees attend to the tension between the church as the body of Christ and the church as a building in need of maintenance, repair, and renovation. Sometimes two or three of these tasks are the responsibility of a single board of trustees, who are charged with all the financial decision making for a congregation. Such boards can be very powerful groups, and as such, they need to cultivate a tremendous sense of accountability to God and the congregations they serve.

The following resources specifically address financial issues that arise in congregational life. However, several of the resources for church councils and executive boards in chapter 4, as well as resources 5 and 6 in chapter 8, are pertinent to the work of stewardship, finance, and property committees. The overarching goal of all three of these committees ought to be their good stewardship of the church's resources in accordance with the gospel. To do this work faithfully, committee members will need to study and pray about the vision and mission of the church as a whole and cultivate healthy interactions among all those whose contributions and commitments they manage.

+ + +

Resource 1 *Motivations for giving*

Stewardship campaigns have long depended on guilt and obligation to motivate the giving of church members. Rightly or wrongly, such tactics have worked in past instances, but many stewardship boards know that their efficacy has expired. People who give grudgingly tend to give as little as possible, parceling out their contributions in small bits to every organization that requests something of them.

Congregations struggle to keep their operating budgets in the black because declining membership and smaller donations mean less money is available to support church staff, programming, and building maintenance at a time when costs for such things have remained level or have risen. Stewardship, finance, and property committees who want to help church members discover motivations for giving that are more positive and compelling than the old duty-bound reasons might explore Paul's teachings on financial giving in his second letter to the Corinthians.

BIBLE STUDY

Have one person read aloud *2 Corinthians 8:1–12.* Note that the specific context for this passage was Paul's effort to take up a relief offering for the Jerusalem church, which was suffering persecution. Discuss the following questions, using the interpretive notes to guide your conversation if necessary.

1. What are the various motivations for giving that Paul cites?

vv. 1–2   Following the examples of other churches/ Christians

vv. 3–4   Defining voluntary giving as an important ministry; need of others

v. 5   Continuation of one's commitment to God

v. 6   Responding to the request of another
v. 7   Consistency with other religious practices
v. 8   Sign of genuine love as compared with others'
            responses
v. 9   Following Christ's example
vv. 10–11 Finishing what one has begun
vv. 11–12 Eagerness to share what one has

2. Which of these motivations might move us (and other church members) to give?
3. How might we communicate these motivations to others over the next months?

Pray for the members of your congregation, that they might embrace reasons for giving that are meaningful, and promote their glad participation in financing the ministries of your church.

Options

For groups new to Bible study, list the various motivations for giving on a sheet of newsprint posted on the wall. Cover the list with another sheet of paper so that you can control what is revealed and what is hidden. Guide the group through a discussion of question 1 by asking the group to focus on each verse or set of verses in turn and the motivations shown on the list for that section of the passage. Work your way through the list, adding or modifying the motivations listed as the group discussion warrants.

This study also works well as a preamble to stewardship, finance, or property committee members' making their own financial pledges to the church's ministries. Study the passage together, then distribute pledge cards and request that each board member silently reread the passage and reflect on his or her own motivations for giving. After a few minutes of silence, ask members to fill out their pledge cards and place them in an offering plate. Offer a prayer of dedication and join in singing the Doxology ("Praise God from Whom All Blessings Flow") or another song of praise appropriate to your congregation's offertory practices.

Resource 2 *Defining our role as stewards*

The term *stewardship* is primarily a "church word," for it has little meaning for people outside congregational life. Few people think of themselves as "stewards" or discuss with others the "stewardship" of particular resources. Instead, our culture uses the terms *manager* and *management* to describe persons and their use of money, property, and other resources. While these terms are helpful in translating religious words into more recognizable ideas, they can also limit the ways in which church members think about stewardship. Finance, property, and stewardship committees can maintain a broader perspective by bringing the cultural image of a "manager" into conversation with the biblical image of a "steward."

INTRODUCTION

Ask participants to think of synonyms for the word *steward*. (Such synonyms might include *manager, overseer, servant,* etc.) Invite them to share any examples of places where the word *steward* is used outside church life. Suggest that the gospel of Luke can help us figure out which of these synonyms and/or examples might be most helpful in our search to understand what a good steward might look like today.

BIBLE STUDY

Read *Luke 12:42–48*. If participants remark on the "beatings" mentioned in verses 47–48, note that these references to physical punishment underscore the immense importance of the steward's role in the eyes of Jesus and his culture. (If no one raises this issue initially, then hold this remark until you are working through that section of the passage.) Discuss the following questions:

1. What is the role of the steward or manager (NRSV)? (Pay attention both to verse 42 and verses 47–48 when answering this question. With regard to the latter verses, you may wish to ask, How might a good steward avoid any beating at all?)
2. What role must the steward (NRSV: slave) avoid?
3. How are we called to be stewards as individuals and as a congregation?
4. What would be poor stewardship on our part?
5. How might we instill a vision of good stewardship in our congregation?

Pray that your board, as a steward of the congregation's resources, might be faithful and prudent in seeking God's will and doing it.

Options

Stewardship committees might use question 5 to guide the creation of an annual stewardship campaign or an ongoing stewardship education process. Finance committees might use their responses to these questions as a norm against which to test the congregation's investment and/or budgetary processes. Property committees might do the same with their answers and the congregation's property use, maintenance, and repair policies.

Resource 3 *The importance of cheerful generosity*

Even in times of economic abundance, most churches operate from a presumption of scarcity. We think that we don't have enough resources to meet all our present and future needs, so we are careful in our allocation of funds, and we guard our endowments with great care. We should not be too surprised, then, that church members feel the same way about their personal finances. They, too, want to make prudent decisions about how they spend their money and how much they save for "rainy days," college educations for offspring, and/or retirement. Few congregations or individuals associate a feeling of cheerfulness with giving, although many have heard the admonishment that "God loves a cheerful giver." The following study explores the concept of generosity and challenges both individuals and stewardship, finance, and property committees to rethink the relationship between cheerful giving and financial security.

SINGING

Join in singing an offertory hymn such as "We Give Thee but Thine Own" (*CH*, 382) or "Take My Gifts" (*CH*, 381; *NCH*, 562). Ask participants whether the hymn they sang represents their perspective on giving and how closely it mirrors their own feelings about the act of giving. Avoid judging people's responses as more or less "orthodox" or correct; instead, encourage participants to assess honestly their emotional and intellectual relationships with the words of the hymn.

BIBLE STUDY

Read *2 Corinthians 9:6–12*, with one voice reading the bulk of the passage and a second voice reading the quotation from Psalm 112 in verse 9. Note that many people may have heard the phrase "God loves a cheerful giver" before. Ask participants to explore with you what being a cheerful giver might mean. Some issues for discussion include,

1. What is the relationship between sowing (giving) and reaping (future benefit)?
2. From where do we get resources that we might choose to share with others?
3. How will we be enriched because of our giving?
4. How does God use our giving to accomplish God's purposes?
5. Why, then, might we enjoy giving?

Pray and ask God's help in spreading the good news that our generosity will bring joy because of the ways it involves us in God's work.

Options

Committees struggling with financial difficulties might explore God's promise of abundant provision carefully to discern how God is providing for their congregations in other ways and how these nonmonetary resources might be put to use for the flourishing of the faith community. These groups might include the question, What are our congregation's resources? Property boards might then pursue donations of materials and labor to address maintenance and repair needs. Stewardship and finance committees might become stewards of volunteer assistants, who substitute their skills for purchased services.

This resource also works well in reverse. Begin with the Bible study, then sing a hymn as an act of worship and affirmation. Suggest that your congregation sing part or all of this hymn as an invitation or offertory response several times throughout the year, or include this hymn in your stewardship campaign process.

Resource 4 *Maintaining an honest perspective*

Roger Fisher and Scott Brown, in their book *Getting Together: Building Relationships As We Negotiate* (Penguin Books, 1988), point out how easily individuals and institutions are misled by their perceptions of a situation. Noting that people tend to focus on information that upholds prior beliefs or concerns, they reflect on the ways that such biased perceptions can hinder problem solving. Many stewardship, finance, and property boards have worked with church members whose perceptions about the church budget, giving expectations, the endowment, or building maintenance seem to contradict those same members' stated hopes for the church's life and mission. Exploring the contours and implications of this tension between contradictory expectations will help committees guide these church members toward a more holistic and constructive perspective.

INTRODUCTION

Tell the following story, which has circulated among church newsletters for several years.

A lay leader of a congregation stood before the people and reported, "I have some bad news, some good news, and then more bad news. It is bad news that the roof must be replaced. The good news is that we have the money to do it. The rest of the bad news is that the money is in your purses, wallets, and checkbooks. We need to motivate your giving it in order to fix the roof."

Ask participants what they think of this story. Is it an accurate picture of the church's perspective on fundraising? Should it be? Why or why not?

BIBLE STUDY

Read *Acts 4:32—5:11*, with different people playing the parts of the narrator, Peter, and Sapphira. Discuss the following questions:

1. Why did the early church practice common ownership of possessions? (See Acts 2:43–45 if you need help answering this question.)
2. What did Ananias and Sapphira do wrong? (See 5:4.)
3. What other choices could Ananias and Sapphira have made? (Did they get in trouble for wanting to keep some of the money or for misrepresenting their resources and intentions?)
4. How are we tempted "to put the Spirit of the Lord to the test" about our resources and our decisions regarding the use of our resources?
5. How are our decisions about giving related to our relationships with God and other people?
6. How does Ananias and Sapphira's situation challenge us to respond to the dilemma posed by the story of the leaking roof?

Pray that your congregation, through the work of your committee, will learn to see the fruitful connections between their personal resources and the resources of a church body made up of individual members.

Options

Many people struggle with the harsh punishment bestowed on Ananias and Sapphira, particularly since the idea of selling all our possessions and giving the proceeds to the church is a generally unappealing idea today. If participants seem lost in this struggle, remind them that the reason for condemnation is not the desire to retain personal property, but the attempt to deceive the community about one's resources and commitment. Talk about the impact of deceit on community life and remind one another of times deceitfulness has threatened the well-being of your congregation. Then brainstorm together ways in which your congregation can honor the fact that the church is not a building, but a community of people, called to share their resources honestly for the good of all.

Some groups prefer to study the scriptures before raising questions of contemporary relevance. To reverse the order of the Bible study and the leaky roof story, begin with the scripture reading and then insert the story before asking question 6.

Resource 5   *Discerning the right time for a building campaign*

Considering a proposal to renovate, expand, or replace a church building generates both excitement and anxiety among church members. Such work calls for large sums of money and major disruptions in the operational life of the congregation. Members may disagree about the need for change and the means of funding those changes. Some members may disagree so vehemently with the plans that they threaten to leave if the building project takes place. Others make similar threats tied to the congregation's refusal to move forward with a project. Sometimes the appropriate questions for determining whether to proceed or not can get lost in the emotional roller coaster of the debate. Turning to the story of how the first Jewish temple came to be built can help stewardship, finance, and property committees clarify the questions the congregation should ask as it makes its decision.

INTRODUCTION

Note that there are many ways to make a decision about whether or not to support a building campaign. These ways include

1. applying personal experiences with finances and common sense,
2. adhering to a set of business principles that the group or some individual considers important,
3. employing conflict-management strategies to resolve disagreements,
4. appealing to the traditions of the congregation, and
5. seeking to discern God's expectations.

State that all these ways make important contributions to the process. Invite participants to engage in the following Bible study as one piece among the many pieces in the deliberation process.

BIBLE STUDY

Observe that the story offered for study resonates with the current issue of the proposed building project, but it does not offer one right answer or position on the issue of whether to pursue the project. State that the story actually offers at least three possible responses—representing three common perspectives on building projects—and that the group will explore all of them.

Ask someone to read aloud *2 Samuel 7:1–3*. Offer the following commentary:

Here we get the issue: David thinks God needs a nice temple, and the religious leader of the time, Nathan, thinks that David's idea is a good one as well. In our circumstances, we want to have a nice (new) church (addition), and [*name person or committee behind building project proposal*—or: "our religious leaders on this one"] think that's a good idea.

Now ask someone to read aloud *2 Samuel 7:4–7*. Summarize this passage as follows:

God says, "Where did you ever get such a crazy idea?! I don't need a temple!" The point seems to be that the old system still works, so don't start trying to fix something that's not really broken.

Continue the story by asking someone to read *2 Samuel 7:8–13*. Summarize this section with these or similar words:

It seems that God has other plans for the community first. The temple idea is simply premature; it needs to be postponed. Other issues are more important now.

Ask participants to respond to your interpretation of the story so far. Do they think you have accurately represented what is going on? What else would they say about the reasons given for not building the temple at that time?

Conclude the story by asking someone to turn to *1 Kings 5:1–5* and read it aloud. Finish your commentary by observing,

Okay, now the message is that the time has come to build. Working on a new building for worship and study has become the right priority.

DISCERNMENT EXERCISE

Invite participants to think about the congregation's building project proposal in light of three questions derived from the scriptural account of the temple building process. Unveil a sheet of newsprint containing the questions at the end of this paragraph. Read the questions aloud, then ask everyone to pause for a few minutes of silent prayer and reflection. After keeping silent for three to five minutes, discuss the questions as a group.

1. Are we getting ahead of ourselves with this project when we have a system that works?
2. Are there other, more important issues that need attention first?
3. Are we living in the time of means and opportunity for building?

Use your answers to the questions to help the committee decide whether to initiate or continue promoting the building project, or whether to wait for a more appropriate time to pursue this change.

Options

Groups throughout a congregation could use this study and exercise to discern their perspectives on a proposed building project. The three questions could be posted on separate sheets of newsprint, and participants could list their responses to each question underneath. Then the committee charged with overseeing the proposal could gather the sheets from each participating group and use that information in the discernment process.

A stewardship, finance, or property committee also might present its decision about a proposal to an executive board, church council, or congregational meeting, using this framework. The committee members could explain how the story helped sharpen their awareness of the options and then could offer their answers to the three questions. Once the committee has made its case, the board, council, or congregation could decide that the committee's rationales are persuasive or could offer alternative responses to the questions that challenge the committee's conclusions.

Chapter 10

Asking God to Serve on the Worship and Altar Committees

Worship is the central act of church life. It is a "service," a work done by God's people to glorify and praise their Creator, Redeemer, and Sustainer. It is an event where God's people are served as well, where God speaks, nourishes, comforts, and blesses all those who gather in God's name. Worship is a time of celebration, a time of remembering God's past actions, experiencing God's present kindness, and proclaiming our hope for the future realization of God's realm in all its fullness. Through the ritual of worship, we are forgiven our failures and reformed in Christ's likeness, that we might go again into the world as the body of Christ.

The primary purpose of a worship or altar committee is to help create a context in which its particular community of faith can engage in meaningful worship. To accomplish this task, worship and altar boards need to educate the congregation about the nature and purposes of worship, participate in worship planning, and provide support for the actual services of worship conducted in their congregations. These committees work closely with church staff and lay worship leaders to shape the liturgical life of their congregations in ways that are true to the scriptures, the traditions of their heritage, and the needs of their communities. They may depend on their denominational book of worship for guidance or work independent of a set liturgy.

Because of the myriad details involved in services of worship, worship and altar board members often lose sight of their primary purpose amid the ordinary tasks assigned them. There is nothing wrong with these committees' spending part of their time setting up for communion, ordering altar flowers, hanging advent greens, recruiting acolytes and lay readers, and/or polishing candlestick holders. In fact, these efforts and others like them contribute greatly to the formative power of the liturgy by creating a rich and hospitable environment for worship and providing appropriate liturgical leadership. Someone needs to purchase the bread and juice or wine for the eucharistic feast and wash the "dishes" afterward! Someone also needs to encourage reflection on the experience of communion so that this important sacrament remains vibrant and meaningful in people's lives. Worship and altar committee members best fulfill their responsibilities when they provide both these services for their congregations.

The challenge facing many worship and altar boards is a lack of understanding among committee members (and their congregations as well) regarding the history and theological significance of the individual aspects of the service of worship. The reasons for including particular items like flowers and pulpit hangings (paraments), the rationale for a particular order of worship, the concept of a liturgical calendar—committee members may not know anything more about these issues than "we've always done it this way" or "that's how they do it at XYZ church." Education about the purposes and practices of worship has to begin with worship and altar committee members, who then can create and interpret meaningful services of worship for their congregations.

Even in congregations in which most of the liturgical leadership resides with ordained clergypersons and worship and altar boards have little influence over the structure and content of worship, the role of interpreter remains an important committee function. Church members need congregational leaders who will teach them the "language" of worship (set prayers, creeds, ritual actions) and encourage them to reflect on what the work of worship means for the rest of their waking hours. This task may be shared with other committees and leaders in the church, but it is rightly the primary task of worship and altar committees to guarantee that such education occurs in ongoing and age-appropriate ways. The work of the worship and altar board goes far beyond readying the worship space for occupancy. It extends to the necessary task of equipping the saints with everything they might need to praise God and receive God's gracious gifts when they gather as the resurrected body of Christ.

+ + +

Resource 1　*The goodness and joy of worship*

There was a time when the focus of Sunday life for Christians was worship, and few other activities were allowed on that day. Farmers might milk their cows and extended families might gather for Sunday dinner, but these necessary or pleasant tasks were planned around the time scheduled for congregational worship. Those days, which were not as idyllic and uncontested as some nostalgic church members claim, are no more. Sporting events, sales at the mall, and family gatherings now compete directly with churches for people's time. Many church members consider regular worship participation to consist of attendance at one or two services a month instead of a weekly habit. They also come expecting to receive certain services from the church without considering what work they are called to do in the service of worship.

Worship and altar committees, then, have to help church members comprehend the people's role in worship. Studying the biblical book of Psalms is helpful in preparing for this task. Many of the biblical psalms are pieces of service music, designed to help people understand and do the work of worship. This resource uses two psalms to help participants explore the goodness and joy of worship.

EXPERIENCING THE PSALMS

Ask participants to sit silently and think about why they gather with other people to worship God. After two minutes of silence, invite participants to stand and read (in unison or responsively) *Psalm 92:1–4*. (Provide Bibles or copies of the text.) Pause for another minute of silent reflection, then invite participants to read (in unison or responsively) *Psalm 150*. Participants may be seated after the second reading.

BIBLE STUDY

Looking closely at both psalms, discuss the following questions:

1. What reasons do the psalmists give for worship?
2. According to these psalms, what attitudes and emotions are reinforced by worship?
3. What are *our* reasons for gathering for worship? How are our reasons similar to and different from the psalmists' reasons?
4. How might regular attendance in worship make a difference in our lives?
5. How might we communicate these reasons to the rest of the congregation?

Conclude the discussion with an enthusiastic unison reading of *Psalm 117*, a short (two-verse) psalm of praise.

Options

Both Psalm 92 and Psalm 150 are contained in most hymnal psalters. Instead of simply reading the psalms, read or chant them with the sung response provided in your hymnal. If silence between scripture readings is an unfamiliar practice in your tradition, take time before beginning this experience to explain the format. Assure participants that you will guide them through the process with quietly spoken instructions.

To expand your committee's study of the psalms and worship, obtain a study Bible and check the margin or footnotes to identify other psalms written specifically for worship. Explore one or two of these psalms each time you gather, using the questions from this resource and other questions developed by members of the committee.

Resource 2 *Worship as a response to God's faithfulness*

The appropriate focus of worship is God. We do not gather to applaud the talent of soloists, although we may indeed give thanks for the gift of music that God has given them. We are not assembled to enforce conformity to a rigid code of liturgical conduct, although we may rightly expect everyone present to honor and revere God in ways appropriate to their ages. Instead, we gather because we take seriously God's commandment to have no other gods before the One who has created, redeemed, and sustained us. Our service of worship allows us to acknowledge and respond to all that God has done. When other concerns begin to obscure this purpose, worship and altar boards can appeal to Psalm 145 to help them and their congregations regain a proper perspective.

BIBLE STUDY

Read *Psalm 145:10–21* responsively, one group taking the even verses and the second group reading the odd verses. (Provide a single biblical translation.) Explain that this psalm, which is attributed to David, is written in the style of an acrostic poem. In the original text, verse one begins with the first letter of the Hebrew alphabet, and each new verse begins with the succeeding letter. Every verse is meant to convey an idea about the character of God and the response of God's people to that character. Explore the psalmist's understanding of the God-human relationship by discussing the following questions:

1. Who does the psalmist say God is? (Pay attention to what the psalmist says God does and translate God's actions into divine attributes.)
2. How does the psalmist say that people will respond to God?
3. Why do God's being and actions warrant this response on the part of God's people?
4. How do our acts of worship imitate the response described by the psalmist?

5. How does our worship fall short of this kind of response?
6. How can we help ourselves and others acknowledge and respond better to God's faithfulness?

Take hands and go around the circle of participants, offering prayers of thankfulness for God's faithfulness. Invite one person to begin the prayer, asking that person to squeeze the hand of the person on his or her right when finished. The person whose hand has been squeezed then contributes her or his prayer, and so on. Tell participants that both spoken and unspoken prayers are welcome. In either case, a squeeze of the next person's hand signals that a prayer has been concluded.

Options

Using the entire text of Psalm 145 offers worship and altar committees even more material for exploring the character of God and the responses we might make to God's faithfulness. Like the psalms in resource 1, this text is also included in some hymnal psalters, so a musical committee could chant the psalm with its sung response. A group unaccustomed to praying aloud could conclude the discussion with a time of silent prayer, following with a prayer spoken by the group leader.

The group could also choose to create its own simple acrostic poem of God's attributes using the alphabet most familiar to them. To engage in this activity, list the letters of the alphabet in order on a piece of newsprint. Then invite participants to suggest words or phrases describing God for each of the letters. Don't forget that God can be described as one who receives certain kinds of responses from people of faith.

Resource 3 *Purposes of a place of worship*

As people accustomed to attending church services, we take for granted the availability of a place of worship. We seldom consider, however, what our church building symbolizes about

God and about our relationship with God. When we debate color schemes for the sanctuary or consider what kind of furnishings are appropriate for that space, we generally consider nothing more than the dictates of good taste and aesthetic preferences. Incorporating the biblical reasons for a place of worship into our redecorating or set-up discussions helps us to balance the shifting standards of interior design with traditional religious concerns for functionality and beauty. Remembering the story of Solomon's dedication of the first temple can help worship and altar committees keep the symbolic and practical purposes of their church building in mind.

INTRODUCTION

Tell participants that the first Jerusalem temple was built by King Solomon, the son of David, and finished in approximately 953 B.C.E. During the traditional new year festival, held to celebrate the fall harvest, Solomon gathered all the people of Israel before the temple altar for a service of dedication. He addressed the people and offered a long prayer of thanksgiving and intercession to God. The reading for today's Bible study comes from Solomon's prayer.

BIBLE STUDY

Ask participants to take turns reading a verse apiece from *1 Kings 8:27–30* and *8:56–61*. Looking carefully back through the passage for ideas, discuss the following questions:

1. How is God present within the temple? (See especially vv. 29 and 57.)
2. Why is God's presence not fully contained within the temple walls?
3. Who besides the people of Israel will know God is near when they see the temple? (See v. 60.)
4. What actions will the presence of the temple call forth from the people? (See especially vv. 30, 58, and 60.)

5. What actions do the people hope their building of the temple will call forth from God?

Ask participants to name ways in which your church building is a sign of God's presence for them. Then list the ways your church building is a sign of God's presence in your local community. Reread *1 Kings 8:57–58* aloud and pray that God's presence with you in your church building will move you to act so that those outside the church walls will know God's presence as well.

Options

Share this resource with the whole congregation by reenacting the temple dedication story as part of your church's kick-off of the programmatic year or its New Year's celebration. Begin with a procession into the sanctuary, with congregational leaders bearing altar items and pulpit/lectern hangings (paraments) to their rightful places. Gather the people before the altar (standing or sitting in the front of the sanctuary) and have a lay leader or pastor play the role of Solomon. Read the scripture passage and have "Solomon" offer a short interpretation of the text crafted from the Bible study questions. Then invite testimonies from participants regarding the symbolic and practical importance of your church building in their lives and the life of your local community. Close with the same rereading and prayer as above.

Resource 4 *A theology of candlelighting*

Many congregations include candles among the symbolic items present in their services of worship. Yet few church members know why candles are part of our worship celebrations, although most would notice if someone took the candles away.

Debates even break out in some congregations over the manner and timing of candlelighting. Should the candles be lit by an usher prior to the service or by youthful acolytes during the prelude? If we're going to have acolytes, how old should they be? Should they wear robes or go without? Worship and altar committees often end up trying to sort through these issues based on practical considerations and insistent voices from the congregation. They unwittingly overlook the theological significance of candlelighting and miss an opportunity to contribute to the formative power of the congregation's liturgical gatherings. A mini-course on this subject can help board members make decisions grounded in both theology and practicality.

A THEOLOGY OF CANDLELIGHTING

Ask participants, Why do you think we light candles in church? Encourage people to share their ideas, even if they seem obvious or silly. Affirm all answers as possibilities. Then suggest the group add to these ideas three reasons suggested by stories or teachings in the Bible.

Tell the group that reason 1 is found in *Genesis 1:1–4*. Read this passage aloud. Ask participants, What was the first thing that God created in the world? Note that light has been around since the beginning of time, and therefore candles in our worship space remind us that God made the world and all that is in it.

Tell the group that reason 2 is found in *Matthew 5:14–16*. Ask someone to read this passage to the group. Note that God wants us to shine like lights in the world. When we do good things, we are acting like God. Ask participants, What good things can we do that will help people see how much God cares about them? After several people have answered, note that candles in our worship space remind us to do these things so that we will be God's lights in the world.

Explain that reason 3 is found in *Exodus 40:1–4*. Read this passage aloud and note that lights have shined in places of worship for as long as such places have existed. We light candles in our churches today to show our connection to all of God's houses throughout history.

Now ask someone to read *Exodus 40:12–14*. Point out that worship leaders have worn robes for a very long time. They are a sign of special duties and also a way of honoring God by dressing up. Ask participants, Which persons wear robes during our services of worship? Discuss whether the role of acolyte, or candlelighter, fits the criteria your congregation has for robed worship leaders, given the theological significance of their task.

Options

This brief theological study is also an excellent format for an acolyte training session. If your congregation decides that children will serve as acolytes, add a few verses of "This Little Light of Mine" after the discussion of reason 2 (Mt. 5:14–16). Following the reading and discussion of Exodus 40:12–14, explain to children that whenever they are scheduled to lead worship by lighting the candles, they honor God when they look their nicest (and, if applicable, when they wear a special robe to show that they have a special job). Emphasize as well that perfection is not the goal; their job is to help the congregation remember who God is (our Creator), what God wants from us (to do good works that shine in the world), and how we are connected to God's people in all times and places (by the continuation of the tradition of candles in worship). Then practice the skills necessary to contribute good leadership as acolytes.

Resource 5 *Role of confession and assurance of pardon in worship*

Included in many worship services is a corporate prayer of confession. Sometimes this prayer is part of the opening work, a way of asking God to forgive again our sinfulness and welcome us into God's house as the prodigal son was welcomed home.

Prayers of confession also fall in the liturgy of communion, where we acknowledge that we come to God's table not because we are strong, but because we are weak and in need of God's sustenance. Both opening and communion prayers of confession require that we make a countercultural admission: We are dependent people in need of grace and assistance to enjoy fruitful and joyous lives. Worship and altar boards can explore together the potentially powerful effect of heartfelt confession during worship through this study of the prophet Isaiah's words and participation in a liturgy of confession and assurance of pardon.

BIBLE STUDY

Ask two people to read *Isaiah 61:1–7,* with the first person taking verses 1–4 and the second person verses 5–7. Then discuss the following questions:

1. What does this text tell us about forgiveness?
2. How are we expected to respond to forgiveness?

LITURGY OF CONFESSION AND ASSURANCE OF PARDON

Invite participants to pray together the following prayer of confession, which draws on common traditional language for such prayers.

Unison:	**Most holy and merciful God:**
	We confess to you and to one another
	that we have sinned by our own fault
	in thought, word, and deed,
	by what we have done,
	and by what we have left undone.
Leader:	We have been deaf to your call to serve as Christ served us.
People:	**Open our hearts, O God.**
Leader:	We have been self-indulgent and have envied those more fortunate than ourselves.
People:	**Open our hearts, O God.**

Leader: We have carried grudges and held on to bitterness over past hurts.

People: **Open our hearts, O God.**

Leader: We have let our fear of failure and pessimism sap our initiative.

People: **Open our hearts, O God, and accept our repentance for the wrongs we have done and the things we have left undone.**

Leader: Restore us, O God. Let your light break forth into the dark places of our hearts, and teach us to be the people you have created us to be.

Unison: **Amen.**

Leader: Through Christ, our light has come, and we have been restored. Let us go about our work in this world, knowing the everlasting joy that God has promised us. We are forgiven!

Unison: **Amen.**

Options

Incorporate this resource into the rhythm of the liturgical year by using it as part of a simple Ash Wednesday service of worship. Following the liturgy of confession and assurance of pardon, make the sign of a cross on the forehead of each participant using ashes made from the previous year's palm branches. (Most liturgical supply houses sell containers of ashes if you cannot or do not wish to make your own.) Say to each person as you make the cross, "Be who God created you to be." Once all have been marked, offer a traditional benediction, such as this one from Numbers 6:24–26:

May God bless you and keep you.
May God's face shine upon you and be gracious unto you.
May God look upon you with kindness and give you peace.

Scripture Index

Luke

1:26–55	84
12:42–48	131
14:12–24	99
16:41–44	80

John

13:1–17	109
11:17–27	126

Acts

2:42–47	44
4:32—5:11	135
5:27–42	58
6:1–6	38
9:36–42	78

Romans

8:35–39	124
12:1–8	67
12:14–21	91
14:7–9	126
16:1–15	108

1 Corinthians

1:4–6	63

2 Corinthians

8:1–12	129
9:6–12	133

Galatians

5:19–23	69

Ephesians

1:17–19	32
4:7	46
4:11–13	46

Philippians

4:10–20	117

Colossians

3:12–17	51

2 Timothy

4:1–5	95

James

1:19–25	43
5:13–16	123

1 Peter

4:7–11	115

Revelation

21:1–4	81
22:1–5	81